**The 50 Cutest Domestic Baby Animals in the World**

## LOCHLAINN SEABROOK WRITES IN THE FOLLOWING GENRES

Academic
Adventure
Alternate History
American Civil War
American History
American Politics
American South
American West
Anatomy and Physiology
Ancient History
Antiquities
Anthologies
Anthropology
Apocrypha
Aquariology
Archaeology
Art
Art History
Astronomy
Aviation
Aviation History
Behavioral Science
Biblical Exegesis
Biblical Hermeneutics
Bioarchaeology
Biography
Book History
Botany
Camping
Children's Books
Christian Mysticism
Citizen's Rights Education
Civil Liberties
Civil Rights Law
Civil Self Defense
Clinical Studies
Coffee Table Books
Coloring Books
Comparative History
Comparative Mythology
Comparative Religion
Conservation
Constitutional Law
Constitutional Studies
Cooking
Criminal Justice
Criminal Procedure
Cryptozoology
Cultural Anthropology
Cultural Geography
Cultural Heritage
Cultural Heritage Studies
Cultural History
Cultural Studies
Cultural Tourism
Deep Time Natural History
Destination Guides
Diet and Nutrition
Earth Sciences
Ecology

Ecotourism
Educational
Encyclopediography
Entertainment
Environmental History
Environmental Science
Environmental Studies
Environmental Tourism
Epistemology
Ethnobotany
Ethnology
Ethology
Ethnomusicology
Ethnic Studies
Etymology
European History
Evolutionary Anthropology
Evolutionary Biology
Evolutionary History
Evolutionary Psychology
Exploration
Exobiology
Exposés
Family Histories
Field Guides
Film
Folklore
Forestry
Genealogy
General Audience
Geography
Geology
Genetics
Ghost Stories
Gospels
Guidebooks
Handbooks
Health and Fitness
Heritage Conservation
Heritage Travel
Hiking
Historical Ecology
Historical Fiction
Historical Nonfiction
Historiography
History
History of Ideas
History of Medicine
History of Science
Hobbies and Crafts
Human Evolution
Humanities
Humor
Ichthyology
Illustrated Lost History
Illustrations
Inspirational
Illustrated Zoological Anthologies
Intellectual History

Interdisciplinary Lost Knowledge
Interviews
Journalism
Law Enforcement
Law of Attraction
Legal Studies
Lexicography
Life After Death
Lifestyle
Literary History
Literature
Lost Intellectual Heritage
Lost Knowledge Studies
Lost Treasures
Marine Biology
Matriarchy
Medical History
Memoir
Men's Studies
Metahistory
Metaphysics
Military
Military History
Museum Studies
Mysteries and Enigmas
Mysticism
Mythology
National Parks
Natural Health
Natural History
Natural Philosophy
Natural Science
Nature
Nature Appreciation
Nature Art
Nonfiction
Oceanography
Onomastics
Outdoor Recreation
Paleoanthropology
Paleoecology
Paleography
Paleoichthyology
Paleontology
Paleozoology
Paranormal
Parapsychology
Parks & Campgrounds
Patriarchy
Patriotism
Performing Arts
Philosophy
Philosophy of Science
Photography
Physical Anthropology
Pictorial
Poetry
Police Studies
Politics

Practical Law
Prehistoric Art
Prehistoric Life
Prehistory
Preservation Studies
Presidential History
Primatology
Primary Documents
Prophecy
Psychology
Public Safety
Quiz
Quotations
Recollections
Reference
Religion
Revolutionary Period
Science
Scripture
Self-help
Social Sciences
Sociology
Southern Culture
Southern Heritage
Southern Narratives
Southern Studies
Southern Traditions
Speeches
Spirituality
Spiritualism
Sport Science
Symbolism
Technology
Thanatology
Thealogy
Theology
Theosophy
Tourism
Travel
UFOlogy
United States
Vanished Works Studies
Vexillology
Victorian Era Studies
Victorian Medicine
Visual Arts
Visual Cultural Memory Studies
Visual Encyclopediography
Visual Natural History
War
Western Civilization
Wildlife
Wildlife Biology
Wildlife Photography
Women's Studies
World History
Writing
Young Adult
Zoology

*Mr. Seabrook does not author books for fame and glory, but for the love of writing and sharing his knowledge.*

**Be curious, not judgmental.**

# The 50 Cutest
# DOMESTIC
# BABY ANIMALS
### In The World

*An Illustrated Guide to Our Most Adorable Young Creatures*

## LOCHLAINN SEABROOK
Bestselling Author, Award-winning Historian, Acclaimed Artist

Diligently Researched and Generously Illustrated
by the Author for the Elucidation of the Reader

2025

Sea Raven Press, Park County, Wyoming USA

THE 50 CUTEST DOMESTIC BABY ANIMALS IN THE WORLD

Published by
Sea Raven Press, LLC, founded 1995
Park County, Wyoming, USA
SeaRavenPress.com

All text, artwork, and illustrations copyright © Lochlainn Seabrook 2025
in accordance with U.S. and international copyright laws and regulations, as stated and protected under the Berne Union for the Protection of Literary and Artistic Property (Berne Convention), and the Universal Copyright Convention (the UCC). All rights reserved under the Pan-American and International Copyright Conventions.

PRINTING HISTORY
1st SRP paperback edition, 1st printing, December 2025 • ISBN: 978-1-955351-82-9
1st SRP hardcover edition, 1st printing, December 2025 • ISBN: 978-1-955351-83-6

## ISBN: 978-1-955351-82-9 (paperback)
Library of Congress Control Number: 2026933223

This work is the copyrighted intellectual property of Lochlainn Seabrook and has been registered with the Copyright Office at the Library of Congress in Washington, D.C., USA. No part of this work (including text, covers, drawings, photos, illustrations, maps, images, diagrams, etc.), in whole or in part, may be used, reproduced, stored in a retrieval system, or transmitted, in any form or by any means now known or hereafter invented, without written permission from the publisher. The sale, duplication, hire, lending, copying, digitalization, or reproduction of this material, in any manner or form whatsoever, is also prohibited, and is a violation of federal, civil, and digital copyright law, which provides severe civil and criminal penalties for any violations.

The 50 Cutest Domestic Baby Animals in the World: An Illustrated Guide to Our Most Adorable Young Creatures, by Lochlainn Seabrook. Includes an introduction, educational section, notes to the reader, and illustrations.

### ARTWORK
Front and back cover design and art, book design, layout, font selection, and interior art by Lochlainn Seabrook.
All images, pictures, photos, illustrations, image captions, graphic design, and graphic art copyright © Lochlainn Seabrook.
All images created and/or selected, placed, manipulated, cleaned, colored, and tinted by Lochlainn Seabrook.
Cover image: "Appaloosa Foal at Play," copyright © Lochlainn Seabrook.
All rights reserved.

All persons who approve of the authority and principles of Colonel Lochlainn Seabrook's literary work, and realize its benefits as a means of reeducating the world about facts left out of mainstream books, are hereby requested to avidly recommend his titles to others and to vigorously cooperate in extending their reach, scope, and influence around the globe.

The views documented in this book concerning domestic baby animals are those of the publisher.
PROUDLY WRITTEN, DESIGNED, AND PUBLISHED IN THE UNITED STATES OF AMERICA.

# Dedication

*To all the animals who share our lives and make the world better by being in it.*

Golden retriever puppy. Illustration copyright © Lochlainn Seabrook.

# Epigraph

"While domestic animals are the product of thousands of years of human engineering, they remain fragile, independent, living beings that deserve our respect, care, and love."

Lochlainn Seabrook 2025

Clydesdale mare and foal. Illustration copyright © Lochlainn Seabrook.

# CONTENTS

*Notes to the Reader* ❧ page 11
*The Benefits of Owning & Caring for Domestic Baby Animals* ❧ page 12
*Introduction, by Lochlainn Seabrook* ❧ page 13

1. Alpaca ❧ page 16
2. Appaloosa Horse ❧ page 18
3. Axolotl ❧ page 20
4. Basset Hound ❧ page 22
5. Bearded Dragon ❧ page 24
6. Border Collie ❧ page 26
7. Burmese Python ❧ page 28
8. Camel ❧ page 30
9. Cavalier King Charles Spaniel ❧ page 32
10. Chinchilla ❧ page 34
11. Clydesdale Horse ❧ page 36
12. Cow ❧ page 38
13. Donkey ❧ page 40
14. Duck ❧ page 42
15. Dwarf Rabbit ❧ page 44
16. Ferret ❧ page 46
17. Flemish Giant Rabbit ❧ page 48
18. French Bulldog ❧ page 50
19. Golden Retriever ❧ page 52
20. Goldfish ❧ page 54
21. Goose ❧ page 56
22. Guinea Pig ❧ page 58
23. Hamster ❧ page 60
24. Hedgehog ❧ page 62
25. Highland Cattle ❧ page 64
26. Himalayan Cat ❧ page 66
27. Jersey Cattle ❧ page 68
28. Llama ❧ page 70
29. Maine Coon Cat ❧ page 72
30. Miniature Donkey ❧ page 74
31. Miniature Horse ❧ page 76
32. Mini Lop Rabbit ❧ page ❧ page 78
33. Mule ❧ page 80
34. Norwegian Forest Cat ❧ page 82
35. Orpington Chicken ❧ page 84
36. Parakeet ❧ page 86
37. Peking Duck ❧ page 88
38. Persian Cat ❧ page 90

39. Pig ꙮ page 92
40. Pygmy Goat ꙮ page 94
41. Quail ꙮ page 96
42. Ragdoll Cat ꙮ page 98
43. Sheep ꙮ page 100
44. Shetland Pony ꙮ page 102
45. Silkie Chicken ꙮ page 104
46. Tortoise ꙮ page 106
47. Turkey ꙮ page 108
48. Welsh Pony ꙮ page 110
49. Yak ꙮ page 112
50. Yorkshire Terrier ꙮ page 114

*Meet the Author-Historian-Artist* ꙮ page 117
*Praise for the Author* ꙮ page 119
*Learn More* ꙮ page 123

Alpaca cria. Illustration copyright © Lochlainn Seabrook.

# Notes to the Reader

MY SOURCES
☛ In keeping with all of my natural history and animal-focused works, this volume is based on reliable, well-established information drawn from veterinary science, animal husbandry references, breed registries, and professional agricultural and zoological sources. Care has been taken to present accurate, balanced descriptions while avoiding exaggeration, sentimentality, or unsupported claims.

MY RESEARCH
☛ Domestic animals vary widely by breed, environment, and individual development. As a result, characteristics such as size, growth rate, temperament, and appearance may differ from one animal to another. Where ranges or averages are provided, they reflect commonly accepted standards rather than absolute values, and are intended to give readers a general understanding rather than rigid definitions.

AGE & DEVELOPMENT
☛ The animals featured in this book are presented during their earliest stages of life, when physical proportions, behavior, and appearance can change rapidly. Descriptions focus on typical traits observed during infancy and early juvenile development, recognizing that each animal matures at its own pace depending on numerous factors, including genetics, care, and surroundings.

TERMINOLOGY
☛ The term "domesticated" is used in this book in its common, everyday sense. While the majority of the animals featured here have been selectively bred by humans over many generations, a small number are naturally wild species that are commonly kept as household pets. These animals are included because of their long-standing and familiar presence in human homes—even though they are not genetically domesticated in the strict biological sense.

ILLUSTRATIONS
☛ All illustrations in this book are artistic interpretations intended to capture the essential features, proportions, and expressions of each young animal. While grounded in anatomical accuracy, these images are not intended to replace photographs or serve as identification tools, but rather to celebrate the beauty, character, and individuality of domestic animal young through visual storytelling.

ANIMAL CARE DISCLAIMER
☛ Neither the author nor the publisher are veterinarians, and this book is not intended as a veterinary manual. It is a general education work and should not be used as a substitute for professional animal care, medical advice, diagnosis, or treatment. Health, nutrition, and care requirements vary by species, breed, age, and individual circumstance. Neither the author nor the publisher assumes responsibility for outcomes resulting from the use or misuse of information contained in this book. Readers should always consult licensed veterinarians, experienced breeders, or other qualified animal professionals when making specific care or health decisions, and local laws and animal welfare standards also need to be followed.

ANIMAL WELFARE
☛ Young animals are largely dependent on their human owners and are therefore especially vulnerable, requiring constant, attentive, and informed care. Readers are reminded that cuteness should never overshadow responsibility. Proper housing, nutrition, socialization, and humane treatment are essential to the well-being of all domestic animals, particularly during their earliest stages of life.

CONSERVATION & STEWARDSHIP
☛ Domestic animals share a long and meaningful history with humanity. Understanding their origins, development, and needs fosters respect and responsible stewardship. By learning about these animals with thoughtfulness and accuracy, we strengthen the bond between people and the creatures who have lived and worked alongside us for millennia.

# The Benefits of Owning & Caring for Domestic Baby Animals

Owning and caring for domestic baby animals offers far more than simple companionship or appeal. The steady routines of feeding, cleaning, and calm interaction foster patience, ease stress, and create a quiet sense of purpose. The presence of a young animal introduces intention into the day, gently anchoring attention in the present moment. These early duties slow everyday life, encouraging focus, consistency, and emotional steadiness in ways few modern pursuits can provide.

Beyond personal benefit, caring for young animals reflects a long human bond with domesticated species—one grounded in trust, reliance, and shared adaptation. This relationship is not accidental, but earned through time, care, and reciprocity. From early farming societies to present-day homes and ranches, raising animals has shaped human values as much as it has shaped human culture. Learning about their needs from the outset deepens respect for the commitment animal ownership demands and underscores how responsible care supports health and longevity.

For children, the experience is especially influential. Helping care for young animals teaches empathy, responsibility, and respect for life. Seeing an animal grow through attentive care reinforces the understanding that living beings are neither disposable nor decorative, but deserving of protection, stability, and compassion. These lessons often carry into adulthood, shaping views on stewardship, obligation, and ethical choice.

In a world increasingly shaped by screens, young animals reconnect us with the physical world. Their warmth, curiosity, and dependence require attention rather than distraction. Caring for them promotes hands-on involvement, sharpens observation, and restores a sense of connection grounded in touch, patience, and deliberate presence—qualities vital to emotional well-being and human growth.

Domestic animals are inseparable from the human story. For thousands of years they have shared our homes, land, and daily work, influencing societies across the world. By learning to care for them—especially during their most vulnerable stages—we honor that lasting partnership. Responsible ownership ensures this bond remains humane, meaningful, and worthy of being carried forward.

In nurturing young animals with care and understanding, we strengthen our own capacity for compassion and discipline, as well as respect for life. Few experiences unite joy with responsibility, or affection with duty, so powerfully. L.S.

# INTRODUCTION

I have spent most of my life observing animals—not only how they look, but how they live. As a naturalist, nature writer, artist, and photographer, my work has always been rooted in close, patient attention to the living world. Over the decades, I've studied wildlife and domestic animals alike, watching how they grow, adapt, and respond to the environments and people around them. Of all the stages of animal life, the earliest has always struck me as the most revealing. It is a time when instinct, vulnerability, and the foundations of behavior are quietly taking shape.

Domestic baby animals are often admired for their charm, yet rarely understood beyond it. They are not decorations or accessories. They are living beings at the very beginning of long, complex lives—lives shaped by care, environment, and human responsibility. Their proportions, movements, and expressions may seem endearing at first glance, but they also tell deeper stories. Within those early traits lie clues to evolutionary history, breed development, and the beginnings of temperament and behavior. To look closely is to see more than cuteness; it is to witness life in one of its most formative moments.

This book was not written to sentimentalize young animals, but to present them clearly and thoughtfully. Each species and breed develops at its own pace, shaped by purpose, history, and its long relationship with humanity. Together, these animals form a living record of domestication—one built through agriculture, companionship, work, and trust across thousands of years. Their earliest days offer insight into that shared history and into the responsibilities that come with it.

*The 50 Cutest Domestic Baby Animals in the World* is not a novelty collection or a children's picture book. It is a visual field guide to early animal life, created with care, respect, and responsible research. It celebrates young mammals, young birds, and young fish without exaggeration, to encourage understanding rather than impulse, and to remind readers that admiration carries with it an obligation of stewardship. When appreciation is matched with knowledge and compassion, our relationship with animals becomes deeper and more meaningful. It is my hope that readers will find both insight and lasting value within these pages.

Lochlainn Seabrook
Park County, Wyoming, USA
January 2026

"Books invite all; they constrain none."
Hartley Burr Alexander (1873-1939)

# The 50 Cutest
# DOMESTIC BABY ANIMALS
### in the World

# ALPACA

COMMON NAME: Alpaca.
BABY NAME: Cria.
SCIENTIFIC NAME: *Vicugna pacos*.
ANIMAL TYPE: Domestic mammal.
TAXONOMIC ORDER: Artiodactyla.
ORIGIN: Central Andes of Peru, Bolivia, and Chile.
DESCRIPTION: Alpaca crias are compact, upright-bodied young camelids with soft fleece that begins forming its characteristic structure within days of birth. Their proportions include a straight neck, slender legs, a small triangular head, and bright, alert eyes. Crias stay close to their mothers and learn social behavior from the herd, depending on adults for protection and guidance. Their early fleece develops either the dense, crimped Huacaya form or the silky, hanging Suri form, both providing insulation suited to high-altitude climates. During this stage they also begin practicing play runs, strengthening coordination and social bonding within the group as they mature during early development.
SIZE: Newborn crias average 12–20 lb and stand 18–24 in tall, typically reaching 40–60 lb by weaning.
APPEARANCE: Rounded head, short muzzle, upright posture, and developing fleece in white, brown, black, gray, or multicolored patterns.
TEMPERAMENT: Gentle, quiet, observant, and strongly herd-oriented, with confidence improving through calm interaction and regular human handling.
CARE REQUIREMENTS: Provide shelter from severe weather, rotational pasture, clean water, and shearing as fleece develops. Veterinary care emphasizes parasite control, nutrition, and close monitoring during the first weeks. Crias benefit from gradual weaning and consistent handling routines.
LIFESPAN: Alpacas typically live 15–20 years.
DOMESTIC ROLE: Fiber-producing livestock valued for soft, hypoallergenic fleece; also used in agritourism, therapy programs, and small-farm settings.
NOTABLE BREEDS / VARIETIES: Huacaya and Suri, differing in fleece structure, density, and texture.
INTERESTING FACTS: Crias stand and walk within an hour of birth. Alpaca fleece contains no lanolin. Alpacas communicate with gentle humming and body posture. Mothers and crias form strong bonds through scent and vocal cues, often recognizing each other by voice alone within the herd environment.

Alpaca cria. Illustration copyright © Lochlainn Seabrook.

# APPALOOSA

COMMON NAME: Appaloosa Horse.
BABY NAME: Foal.
SCIENTIFIC NAME: *Equus ferus caballus*.
ANIMAL TYPE: Domestic mammal.
TAXONOMIC ORDER: Perissodactyla.
ORIGIN: Pacific Northwest of the United States; developed by the Nez Perce people through selective breeding of domestic horses.
DESCRIPTION: Appaloosa foals are sturdy, long-legged baby horses known for early coordination and alert behavior. Within hours of birth, foals are able to stand, walk, and nurse, demonstrating strong instinctive mobility. Their physical development emphasizes balance, endurance, and agility rather than bulk, reflecting the breed's historical use as a versatile riding and travel horse. Appaloosa foals grow rapidly during their first year, developing strong joints and muscular definition suited for sustained movement. Social bonding with the dam and herd begins immediately and plays a major role in behavioral development. Early handling helps reinforce the breed's natural intelligence and responsiveness. Their growth rate is steady, producing a durable adult horse capable of long-term work and riding, even at extended distances across varied terrain and climates.
SIZE: Newborn foals typically weigh 100–130 lb and stand approximately 3–3.5 ft tall at the shoulder.
APPEARANCE: Smooth coat that may appear plain at birth, with spotting, mottling, and color contrast developing as the foal matures.
TEMPERAMENT: Curious, intelligent, and people-aware, with a calm but confident disposition and strong learning ability.
CARE REQUIREMENTS: Require regular nursing, veterinary monitoring, safe pasture, clean shelter, and early hoof and handling care during early developmental stages.
LIFESPAN: Appaloosa horses typically live 25–30 yrs.
DOMESTIC ROLE: Riding, ranch work, sport competition, trail use, and companionship.
NOTABLE BREEDS / VARIETIES: Leopard, blanket, snowflake, and varnish roan coat patterns.
INTERESTING FACTS: Many Appaloosa foals change color dramatically as they grow. The breed is known for striped hooves and mottled skin. Appaloosas were prized for stamina and reliability by early horse cultures, particularly for long-distance travel and diverse terrain in harsh conditions.

Appaloosa horse foal. Illustration copyright © Lochlainn Seabrook.

# AXOLOTL

COMMON NAME: Axolotl.
BABY NAME: Larva.
SCIENTIFIC NAME: *Ambystoma mexicanum*.
ANIMAL TYPE: Domesticated aquatic amphibian.
TAXONOMIC ORDER: Caudata.
ORIGIN: Central Mexico, originally from Lake Xochimilco and Lake Chalco, now maintained almost entirely in captivity.
DESCRIPTION: Axolotl larvae hatch with external gills, soft translucent skin, and underdeveloped limbs. Early life is fully aquatic, with constant suspension in the water column and slow, deliberate movement. Growth is steady, marked by rapid limb formation and increasing coordination within the first few weeks. Unlike most amphibians, axolotls retain larval traits into adulthood, a condition known as neoteny. Babies feed on small aquatic invertebrates and rely heavily on water quality for survival. Their nervous system and sensory organs develop early, allowing quick responses to light and motion. Larvae spend much of their time resting or gently swimming near the substrate. Regenerative abilities are present from a very young age. As juveniles mature, body proportions lengthen while gills remain prominent. Development is strongly influenced by temperature and nutrition.
SIZE: Newly hatched larvae measure about 0.4–0.6 in. and reach 3–5 in. within several mos.
APPEARANCE: Feathery external gills, broad head, small limbs, smooth skin, and a laterally flattened tail.
TEMPERAMENT: Calm, passive, and non-aggressive, with limited social interaction.
CARE REQUIREMENTS: Require cool, clean water, gentle filtration, stable parameters, and appropriate live or prepared foods, such as brine shrimp, finely crushed flakes, or micro-pellets.
LIFESPAN: Axolotls typically live 10–15 yrs in captivity.
DOMESTIC ROLE: Educational species, scientific research animal, and aquarium companion.
NOTABLE BREEDS / VARIETIES: Leucistic, albino, melanoid, wild type, and GFP laboratory strains.
INTERESTING FACTS: Axolotl larvae can regenerate lost limbs, spinal tissue, and parts of the heart. They do not naturally undergo metamorphosis. Their smile-like facial structure is due to skull shape, not expression. Axolotls are critically endangered in the wild. Baby axolotls breathe primarily through external gills. Their regenerative abilities are studied worldwide for medical research.

Axolotl larva. Illustration copyright © Lochlainn Seabrook.

# BASSET HOUND

COMMON NAME: Basset Hound.
BABY NAME: Puppy.
SCIENTIFIC NAME: *Canis lupus familiaris*.
ANIMAL TYPE: Domestic mammal.
TAXONOMIC ORDER: Carnivora.
ORIGIN: France, developed as a low-slung scent hound for tracking small game over long distances.
DESCRIPTION: Basset Hound puppies are heavy-boned, short-legged dogs with oversized features that appear almost comical at birth. Despite their low stature, puppies are surprisingly strong and solid, with dense bone structure evident early in development. Their movement is deliberate rather than quick, reflecting a breed designed for endurance instead of speed. From a young age, Basset puppies show strong scenting behavior, frequently keeping their noses close to the ground. Growth is slow and steady, with joints and muscles developing to support their long bodies. Puppies mature mentally at a relaxed pace, often retaining a playful but stubborn personality. Early social interaction is important to balance independence with responsiveness. The breed's early form closely mirrors its adult silhouette, including loose skin and elongated ears, which become more pronounced with age and movement, especially as coordination improves.
SIZE: Newborn puppies typically weigh 1–2 lb and reach 20–30 lb by 6 mos of age.
APPEARANCE: Long drooping ears, loose wrinkled skin, short legs, and large expressive eyes with a smooth, low-set body.
TEMPERAMENT: Gentle, affectionate, and laid-back, with a curious nose-driven nature and occasional stubbornness.
CARE REQUIREMENTS: Need regular feeding, ear cleaning, joint support, moderate exercise, and patient training.
LIFESPAN: Basset Hounds typically live 10–12 yrs.
DOMESTIC ROLE: Family companion, scent work, tracking, and low-energy household dog.
NOTABLE BREEDS / VARIETIES: Traditional tricolor, lemon and white, and red and white coat variations.
INTERESTING FACTS: Basset puppies have ears long enough to sweep scents toward the nose. Their bone density is among the highest of all dog breeds. The name "Basset" comes from the French word meaning "low." Their loose skin helps trap scent particles, enhancing tracking ability, while their deliberate pace allows careful scent work over long distances without fatigue buildup.

Basset hound puppy. Illustration copyright © Lochlainn Seabrook.

# BEARDED DRAGON

COMMON NAME: Bearded Dragon.
BABY NAME: Hatchling.
SCIENTIFIC NAME: *Pogona vitticeps.*
ANIMAL TYPE: Domestic reptile.
TAXONOMIC ORDER: Squamata.
ORIGIN: Australia, native to arid woodlands and semi-desert regions with open basking areas.
DESCRIPTION: Bearded dragon hatchlings are small, alert reptiles with compact bodies and proportionally large heads at birth. They grow rapidly during the first year, developing strong limbs and a broad, flattened torso suited for basking and ground movement. Hatchlings are active and curious, frequently exploring their enclosure and responding to movement. Their behavior is strongly influenced by temperature, with activity increasing under proper heat and lighting. Young dragons display early instinctive behaviors such as sunning, head bobbing, and territorial posturing. Growth occurs in spurts rather than evenly, requiring frequent feeding and proper nutrition. Hatchlings are visually oriented hunters, tracking live prey with precision. Early handling helps reduce skittishness and encourages calm interaction. As they mature, body proportions widen and the characteristic "beard" becomes more defined. Juveniles begin showing clearer color patterns and social signaling as development progresses. Relaxed exposure to daily routines helps reinforce predictable behavior and environmental tolerance.
SIZE: Hatchlings measure 3–4 in long and may reach 16–24 in as adults.
APPEARANCE: Triangular head, spiky beard scales, rough textured skin, sturdy limbs, and a long tapering tail.
TEMPERAMENT: Calm, alert, and generally docile, with curious behavior and mild territorial displays.
CARE REQUIREMENTS: Require heat gradients, UVB lighting, insect and vegetable diet, hydration, and regular enclosure cleaning.
LIFESPAN: Bearded dragons typically live 8–12 yrs.
DOMESTIC ROLE: Companion reptile, educational pet, and beginner-friendly lizard species.
NOTABLE BREEDS / VARIETIES: Standard, leatherback, hypomelanistic, and translucent morphs.
INTERESTING FACTS: Hatchlings can grow several inches in a single month. Bearded dragons communicate through head bobbing and arm waving. Their "beard" darkens when stressed or excited, often signaling dominance or territorial display.

Bearded dragon hatchling. Illustration copyright © Lochlainn Seabrook.

# BORDER COLLIE

COMMON NAME: Border Collie.
BABY NAME: Puppy.
SCIENTIFIC NAME: *Canis lupus familiaris*.
ANIMAL TYPE: Domestic mammal.
TAXONOMIC ORDER: Carnivora.
ORIGIN: United Kingdom, developed along the England–Scotland border as an advanced sheep-herding dog.
DESCRIPTION: Border Collie puppies are alert, finely built dogs known for exceptional intelligence and intense focus from a very young age. Their bodies are lean rather than bulky, with long limbs already showing agility and balance. Puppies display constant curiosity and problem-solving behavior, often watching movement closely and responding quickly to changes. Even at a few wks old, many show instinctive herding behaviors such as stalking, crouching, and controlled bursts of speed. Energy levels are high, requiring frequent engagement and stimulation. Growth is rapid during the first several mos, with coordination developing alongside muscle tone. Mental development is especially fast, and puppies quickly learn patterns, routines, and commands. Without structure, boredom may appear early. Their physical refinement increases with age rather than mass. Border Collie puppies mature into highly responsive working dogs when properly guided.
SIZE: Newborn puppies weigh about 0.75–1 lb and reach 20–30 lb by 6 mos of age.
APPEARANCE: Slender body, long legs, expressive almond-shaped eyes, and a smooth or lightly feathered coat often in black and white.
TEMPERAMENT: Extremely intelligent, energetic, attentive, and eager to work, with strong focus and sensitivity.
CARE REQUIREMENTS: Require frequent mental stimulation, daily exercise, socialization, training, grooming, and structured routines.
LIFESPAN: Border Collies typically live 12–15 yrs.
DOMESTIC ROLE: Herding livestock, canine sports, working companion, and active family dog.
NOTABLE BREEDS / VARIETIES: Smooth coat and rough coat types with varied markings and colors.
INTERESTING FACTS: Border Collies are widely regarded as the most intelligent of all dog breeds. Puppies often learn commands after only a few repetitions. Their distinctive "herding eye" appears early in development during instinctive play behavior.

Border Collie puppy. Illustration copyright © Lochlainn Seabrook.

# BURMESE PYTHON

COMMON NAME: Burmese Python.
BABY NAME: Hatchling.
SCIENTIFIC NAME: *Python bivittatus*.
ANIMAL TYPE: Constrictor reptile.
TAXONOMIC ORDER: Squamata.
ORIGIN: Southeast Asia, native to forests, grasslands, and wetlands of Myanmar, Thailand, Laos, Cambodia, Vietnam, and China.
DESCRIPTION: Burmese python hatchlings emerge fully formed and independent, measuring several feet in length at birth. They possess strong musculature from the outset, allowing effective movement and prey capture early in life. Unlike mammals, hatchlings receive no parental care after birth and must rely on instinct immediately. Growth during the first year is rapid when food is abundant, with body mass increasing dramatically. Juveniles spend much of their time concealed, using camouflage to avoid predators. Feeding behavior begins within weeks, typically on small mammals or birds. Hatchlings exhibit deliberate movement rather than quick bursts of speed. Their bodies are proportionally slender compared to adults, with less pronounced girth. As they mature, muscle density and body thickness increase steadily. Early development is focused on survival efficiency rather than behavioral complexity.
SIZE: Hatchlings average 18–24 in long and weigh about 3–5 oz at birth.
APPEARANCE: Slender body, smooth glossy scales, dark brown blotches outlined in black on a tan background, with a patterned head.
TEMPERAMENT: Generally calm but alert, defensive when startled, and reactive rather than aggressive.
CARE REQUIREMENTS: Require controlled heat, humidity, secure enclosure, appropriate prey size, and careful handling as growth is rapid.
LIFESPAN: Burmese pythons typically live 20–25 yrs.
DOMESTIC ROLE: Captive exotic reptile, educational specimen, and zoological display animal.
NOTABLE BREEDS / VARIETIES: Albino, granite, labyrinth, green, and selectively bred color morphs.
INTERESTING FACTS: Burmese python hatchlings can double their length within the first year. They shed frequently during growth phases. Despite their size potential, they hatch without venom or parental protection. Juveniles depend on camouflage and rapid feeding to survive early life stages. Invasive in the U.S.

Burmese python hatchling. Illustration copyright © Lochlainn Seabrook.

# CAMEL

COMMON NAME: Camel.
BABY NAME: Calf.
SCIENTIFIC NAME: *Camelus dromedarius*.
ANIMAL TYPE: Domestic mammal.
TAXONOMIC ORDER: Artiodactyla.
ORIGIN: North Africa and the Middle East, domesticated thousands of years ago for transport, milk, meat, and hair fiber.
DESCRIPTION: Camel calves are long-legged, soft-coated young animals born with an alert and curious demeanor. Unlike many domestic mammals, calves are able to stand and walk within hours of birth, a trait essential to survival in harsh desert environments. Their bodies appear lightly built at first, with narrow frames that lengthen rapidly during the first year. Although born without a fully developed hump, the structure begins forming gradually as fat storage increases. Calves rely heavily on maternal milk early on, which is rich in nutrients and antibodies. Growth is steady rather than rapid, with bones and joints strengthening to support adult size and endurance. Young camels are playful and inquisitive, often engaging in short bursts of running and hopping. Social bonding with the mother is strong, and calves remain close for guidance and protection. Early development emphasizes balance, stamina, and environmental awareness rather than speed. Their early proportions already hint at the tall, upright posture of adults.
SIZE: Newborn calves typically weigh 70–100 lb and reach 300–400 lb by 12 mos of age.
APPEARANCE: Slender legs, small developing hump, large eyes, soft woolly coat, and a narrow, gently curved neck.
TEMPERAMENT: Calm, curious, and gentle, with increasing confidence as the calf matures.
CARE REQUIREMENTS: Require maternal nursing, shade, hydration, gradual diet transition, protection from extreme conditions, social bonding, rest, and human supervision.
LIFESPAN: Camels typically live 40–50 yrs.
DOMESTIC ROLE: Pack animal, riding animal, milk producer, hair fiber source, meat source, cultural livestock in arid regions.
NOTABLE BREEDS / VARIETIES: Regional landraces adapted to desert, coastal, and semi-arid environments.
INTERESTING FACTS: Camel calves can close their nostrils against blowing sand. Their milk intake supports muscle development. Hump formation begins months after birth rather than at delivery as fat storage gradually increases.

Camel calf. Illustration copyright © Lochlainn Seabrook.

# CAVALIER KING CHARLES SPANIEL

COMMON NAME: Cavalier King Charles Spaniel.
BABY NAME: Puppy.
SCIENTIFIC NAME: *Canis lupus familiaris.*
ANIMAL TYPE: Domestic mammal.
TAXONOMIC ORDER: Carnivora.
ORIGIN: United Kingdom, bred as a royal companion dog favored by British nobility.
DESCRIPTION: Cavalier King Charles Spaniel puppies are small, soft-bodied dogs with rounded features and an immediately affectionate demeanor. From birth, puppies display a calm and people-oriented nature, often seeking warmth and contact. Their bodies are compact and lightly boned, developing evenly without extreme growth spurts. Movement is gentle and fluid, with a natural elegance that appears early. Puppies mature quickly emotionally, forming strong bonds with caregivers within weeks. Play behavior is mild rather than rough, reflecting the breed's long history as a lap companion. As they grow, facial features remain soft and expressive rather than sharp or angular. Coat texture begins silky and becomes longer with age, particularly on the ears and chest.
SIZE: Newborn puppies typically weigh under 1 lb and reach 10–13 lb by 6 mos of age.
APPEARANCE: Large round eyes, domed head, long feathered ears, short muzzle, and a silky, gently wavy coat.
TEMPERAMENT: Affectionate, gentle, eager to please, and highly social with both humans and other animals.
CARE REQUIREMENTS: Require frequent grooming, consistent feeding, gentle exercise, heart monitoring, and positive training.
LIFESPAN: Cavalier King Charles Spaniels typically live 12–15 yrs.
DOMESTIC ROLE: Companion animal, therapy dog, and affectionate household pet.
NOTABLE BREEDS / VARIETIES: Blenheim, tricolor, ruby, and black and tan coat patterns.
INTERESTING FACTS: The breed is named after England's King Charles II. Puppies are known for maintaining eye contact unusually early. Bred solely for companionship, cavaliers are among the most people-oriented of all the toy breeds, following owners and displaying sensitivity to human emotion and voice. Often described as "velcro dogs" for their love of being with people.

Cavalier King Charles Spaniel puppy. Illustration copyright © Lochlainn Seabrook.

# CHINCHILLA

COMMON NAME: Chinchilla.
BABY NAME: Kit.
SCIENTIFIC NAME: *Chinchilla lanigera*.
ANIMAL TYPE: Domestic mammal.
TAXONOMIC ORDER: Rodentia.
ORIGIN: South America, originally native to the Andes Mountains and later domesticated for companionship and fur.
DESCRIPTION: Chinchilla kits are extremely small, soft-bodied mammals born fully furred with open eyes. Unlike many rodents, kits are precocial and capable of standing and moving shortly after birth. Early movement is cautious and slightly uncoordinated as balance and muscle strength develop. Growth during the first few weeks is steady, with rapid increases in body mass and agility. Kits rely heavily on their mother's milk but begin nibbling solid food within days. Their digestive systems mature slowly and require stable conditions. Social awareness develops early, with kits responding to sounds, motion, and gentle handling. Curiosity is evident even at a young age, though stress sensitivity remains high. As they mature, kits become more agile jumpers with strong hind legs. Development favors coordination and alertness rather than speed. Proper early care is critical due to their delicate physiology and susceptibility to overheating. Environmental stability plays a major role in healthy growth, as kits react strongly to noise, temperature changes, and handling frequency. Consistent routines help reduce stress during early development.
SIZE: Newborn kits weigh about 1.5–2 oz and may reach 1–1.5 lb by 6 mos of age.
APPEARANCE: Dense velvety fur, large rounded ears, prominent dark eyes, short forelimbs, and powerful hind legs.
TEMPERAMENT: Gentle, alert, and cautious, with playful bursts of energy and strong sensitivity to handling.
CARE REQUIREMENTS: Require cool temperatures, dust baths, high-fiber diet, quiet housing, and careful handling.
LIFESPAN: Chinchillas typically live 10–15 yrs.
DOMESTIC ROLE: Companion animal valued for temperament, cleanliness, and unique coat texture.
NOTABLE BREEDS / VARIETIES: Standard gray, beige, ebony, white mosaic, and violet color mutations.
INTERESTING FACTS: Chinchilla fur is among the densest of any mammal. Kits are born with full fur and open eyes. They can overheat easily due to their thick coats. Require dust baths.

Chinchilla kit. Illustration copyright © Lochlainn Seabrook.

# CLYDESDALE HORSE

COMMON NAME: Clydesdale Horse.
BABY NAME: Foal.
SCIENTIFIC NAME: *Equus ferus caballus*.
ANIMAL TYPE: Domestic mammal.
TAXONOMIC ORDER: Perissodactyla.
ORIGIN: Scotland, developed in the Clyde Valley as a powerful draft horse for farm work and hauling heavy loads.
DESCRIPTION: Clydesdale foals are large, long-legged newborns with an immediately noticeable sense of height and balance. Even at birth, their limbs appear sturdy and straight, supporting a frame built for future strength rather than speed. Foals are alert and curious, often standing within hours and following their mothers closely. Their movement is surprisingly coordinated for such a large baby, with an elastic, slightly exaggerated gait. Early growth emphasizes leg length before body mass fills out. Muscles develop gradually, laying the foundation for the breed's renowned pulling power. Foals display gentle social behavior, bonding quickly with both mares and caretakers. Their calm demeanor is evident early, making them easier to handle than many lighter horse breeds. As they mature, their proportions slowly shift from lanky to solid and muscular. The breed's characteristic feathering on the lower legs begins to appear as the foal grows older, along with increased chest width and overall mass. Early exposure to routine care helps reinforce the breed's naturally cooperative temperament.
SIZE: Newborn foals typically weigh 180–220 lb and may reach 1,200–1,400 lb as adults.
APPEARANCE: Tall frame, long legs, broad chest, refined head, and developing feathering on the lower legs.
TEMPERAMENT: Calm, gentle, and people-oriented, with a steady and trusting disposition.
CARE REQUIREMENTS: Require ample space, proper nutrition for growth, hoof care, grooming of leg feathering, and early handling.
LIFESPAN: Clydesdale horses typically live 20–25 yrs.
DOMESTIC ROLE: Agricultural work, ceremonial use, parades, shows, and family farm companionship.
NOTABLE BREEDS / VARIETIES: Bay with white markings is most common, with occasional black, brown, or roan individuals.
INTERESTING FACTS: Clydesdale foals grow rapidly during their first year. The breed is famous for its high-stepping movement. Their leg feathering requires regular care even in youth. Clydesdales mature slowly, reaching full size over several years.

Clydesdale horse foal. Illustration copyright © Lochlainn Seabrook.

# COW

COMMON NAME: Cow.
BABY NAME: Calf.
SCIENTIFIC NAME: *Bos taurus*.
ANIMAL TYPE: Domestic mammal.
TAXONOMIC ORDER: Artiodactyla.
ORIGIN: Domesticated from wild aurochs in Eurasia over 10,000 yrs ago for meat, milk, hides, leather, and labor.
DESCRIPTION: Cow calves are large, long-legged newborns that can stand and walk within hours of birth. Their bodies are proportionally slim at first, with long limbs, narrow hips, and relatively large heads. Early movement appears awkward but quickly becomes steady as muscles strengthen. Calves are highly responsive to their mothers, relying on close contact for warmth, protection, and nourishment. Growth during the first months is rapid, with significant increases in height and weight. Digestive systems develop gradually as calves transition from milk to forage. Social awareness appears early, and calves often form close bonds with herd mates. Vocal communication is frequent, especially between cow and calf. Curiosity increases as coordination improves, leading to playful running and kicking behaviors. Physical proportions slowly shift toward the heavier, broader adult form. Early handling helps calves adapt easily to human care and farm routines.
SIZE: Newborn calves typically weigh 60–100 lb and reach 300–500 lb by 6 mos of age.
APPEARANCE: Large soft eyes, long legs, rounded muzzle, short fine hair, and a slightly oversized head relative to the body.
TEMPERAMENT: Gentle, calm, curious, and socially attentive, with strong bonding instincts toward caretakers and herd members.
CARE REQUIREMENTS: Require regular feeding, clean water, shelter from weather, veterinary monitoring, and gradual dietary transition.
LIFESPAN: Domestic cattle typically live 15–20 yrs.
DOMESTIC ROLE: Livestock for dairy, beef, breeding, leather production, and agricultural sustainability worldwide.
NOTABLE BREEDS / VARIETIES: Holstein, Jersey, Angus, Hereford, Longhorn, Shorthorn, and Highland cattle.
INTERESTING FACTS: Calves recognize their mother's voice shortly after birth. They can run within hours of being born. Cattle have panoramic vision, allowing calves to detect movement across wide areas without turning their heads.

Cow calf. Illustration copyright © Lochlainn Seabrook.

# DONKEY

COMMON NAME: Donkey.
BABY NAME: Foal.
SCIENTIFIC NAME: *Equus africanus asinus*.
ANIMAL TYPE: Domestic mammal.
TAXONOMIC ORDER: Perissodactyla.
ORIGIN: Northeastern Africa, a purebred equine domesticated from wild asses and spread worldwide as a hardy working animal.
DESCRIPTION: Donkey foals are long-legged, fuzzy-coated youngsters with proportionally large ears and alert expressions. At birth, they are able to stand and nurse within a short time, reflecting their evolution in open, predator-prone landscapes. Foals grow steadily rather than rapidly, developing strong bones and dense muscle over time. Their movements are cautious but confident, showing early balance and coordination. Young donkeys are naturally observant and tend to pause before reacting, a trait often mistaken for stubbornness. Vocalization appears early, with foals learning to bray by mimicking adults. Social bonding is strong, and foals form close attachments to their mothers and herd mates. They often seek physical closeness and reassurance during early development. Foals show early curiosity about their surroundings but investigate slowly and deliberately. Growth continues for several years, with full physical maturity reached later than many domestic animals. Early handling shapes trust, confidence, and calm behavior in adulthood. This period strongly influences lifelong temperament.
SIZE: Newborn foals weigh about 20–30 lb and reach 200–300 lb by 1 yr, depending on breed.
APPEARANCE: Soft shaggy coat, long upright ears, slender legs, short mane, and large dark eyes.
TEMPERAMENT: Gentle, cautious, intelligent, and affectionate, with a calm and thoughtful demeanor.
CARE REQUIREMENTS: Require nursing or milk replacer, safe shelter, gradual weaning, hoof care, and social interaction.
LIFESPAN: Donkeys typically live 25–40 yrs.
DOMESTIC ROLE: This distinct equine species serves as a pack animal, farm helper, companion animal, and livestock guardian.
NOTABLE BREEDS / VARIETIES: Standard donkey, miniature donkey, and mammoth donkey.
INTERESTING FACTS: Donkey foals can recognize their mother's bray shortly after birth. Their large ears help regulate body temperature. Donkeys are known for strong long-term memory.

Donkey foal. Illustration copyright © Lochlainn Seabrook.

# DUCK

COMMON NAME: Duck.
BABY NAME: Duckling.
SCIENTIFIC NAME: *Anas platyrhynchos domesticus*.
ANIMAL TYPE: Domestic bird.
TAXONOMIC ORDER: Anseriformes.
ORIGIN: Eurasia, domesticated from wild mallards for eggs, meat, feathers, down, pest control, and utility around human settlements.
DESCRIPTION: Ducklings are small, lightweight birds covered in dense, insulating down rather than feathers. At hatching, they are highly mobile and instinctively follow caregivers, displaying strong imprinting behavior. Their bodies are rounded, with short necks and proportionally large heads that give them a distinctly juvenile appearance. Ducklings grow rapidly during their first weeks, gaining weight and strength daily. Early movement is slightly clumsy on land but confident in shallow water. They rely heavily on warmth, food, and protection during this stage. As growth continues, down is gradually replaced by juvenile feathers. Bill shape and leg placement already reflect adult waterfowl anatomy. Vocalization begins early, with soft peeping used to communicate distress or contentment. Social awareness develops quickly, and ducklings respond strongly to flock movement and sound cues. Development is fast, with major physical changes occurring within the first month.
SIZE: Newly hatched ducklings weigh about 1.5–2.5 oz and may reach 2–5 lb by 8–10 wks, depending on breed.
APPEARANCE: Soft downy plumage, flat bill, webbed feet, short neck, and rounded body with a low center of gravity.
TEMPERAMENT: Social, curious, alert, and gentle, with strong flocking instincts and attachment to caregivers.
CARE REQUIREMENTS: Require constant access to clean water, proper starter feed, warmth, protection from predators, and clean bedding.
LIFESPAN: Domestic ducks typically live 8–12 yrs.
DOMESTIC ROLE: Egg production, meat source, feathers, garden pest control, and companion livestock.
NOTABLE BREEDS / VARIETIES: Pekin, Khaki Campbell, Rouen, Indian Runner, and Cayuga.
INTERESTING FACTS: Ducklings can swim shortly after hatching. They imprint strongly on their mother (or first moving caregiver) within the first day of life. Their waterproofing depends on oils from the preen gland, applied later during feather development.

Duck duckling. Illustration copyright © Lochlainn Seabrook.

# DWARF RABBIT

COMMON NAME: Dwarf Rabbit.
BABY NAME: Kit.
SCIENTIFIC NAME: *Oryctolagus cuniculus*.
ANIMAL TYPE: Domestic mammal.
TAXONOMIC ORDER: Lagomorpha.
ORIGIN: Europe, selectively bred in the 20$^{th}$ Century for small size and compact features.
DESCRIPTION: Dwarf rabbit kits are extremely small, round-bodied mammals characterized by shortened faces and oversized eyes. At birth, kits are hairless and blind, relying entirely on maternal care for warmth and nourishment. Growth during the first weeks is rapid, with fur developing quickly and ears remaining short relative to head size. Movement begins cautiously, progressing from unsteady hops to confident bursts of energy. Dwarf kits display early curiosity and exploratory behavior once mobile. Their skeletal structure is compact, with short limbs and a rounded torso that persists into adulthood. Compared to larger rabbit breeds, dwarf kits retain juvenile proportions longer. Social behaviors emerge early, including grooming motions and gentle nuzzling. Vocalizations are rare, with communication relying mainly on body language. As they mature, kits develop strong spatial awareness and precise movement despite their size. Early handling and environmental enrichment strongly influence confidence and adaptability later in life.
SIZE: Newborn kits weigh about 1–2 oz and reach 1–2.5 lb by adulthood, depending on variety.
APPEARANCE: Very small body, short ears, round head, large eyes, soft dense fur, and compact limbs.
TEMPERAMENT: Gentle, alert, and playful, often curious but cautious, with strong bonding tendencies.
CARE REQUIREMENTS: Require warm nesting early, gradual weaning, high-fiber diet, clean housing, and gentle handling.
LIFESPAN: Dwarf rabbits typically live 8–12 yrs.
DOMESTIC ROLE: Companion animal, educational pet, and small indoor household rabbit.
NOTABLE BREEDS / VARIETIES: Netherland Dwarf, Mini Rex, Mini Lop, and Dwarf Hotot.
INTERESTING FACTS: Dwarf rabbits retain juvenile facial features into adulthood. Rabbits' teeth grow continuously throughout life. Their compact size results from specific dwarfing genes carefully managed by breeders to prevent complications.

Dwarf rabbit kit. Illustration copyright © Lochlainn Seabrook.

# FERRET

COMMON NAME: Ferret.
BABY NAME: Kit.
SCIENTIFIC NAME: *Mustela putorius furo*.
ANIMAL TYPE: Domestic mammal.
TAXONOMIC ORDER: Carnivora.
ORIGIN: Europe, domesticated from the European polecat for hunting rodents and small pests.
DESCRIPTION: Ferret kits are extremely small and underdeveloped at birth, born blind, deaf, and dependent on constant maternal care. During the first weeks, growth is rapid, with limbs lengthening and the spine becoming more flexible. Kits begin opening their eyes at about 4–5 wks, followed shortly by exploratory movement and play behavior. Their bodies elongate early, forming the sleek, tubular shape characteristic of the species. Movement transitions from crawling to bounding hops as muscle coordination improves. Kits are highly social and learn through interaction with littermates. Play-fighting and chasing are essential for healthy behavioral development. Curiosity intensifies as sensory awareness increases. Energy levels rise sharply during juvenile stages, requiring frequent activity. By several mos, kits closely resemble miniature adults in form and behavior.
SIZE: Newborn kits weigh about 0.02–0.06 lb and typically reach 1–3 lb by 6 mos of age.
APPEARANCE: Long slender body, short legs, pointed face, small rounded ears, and soft fine fur that thickens with age.
TEMPERAMENT: Playful, curious, energetic, and highly social, with strong bonding to humans and other ferrets.
CARE REQUIREMENTS: Require high-protein diet, clean enclosure, daily exercise, enrichment toys, routine veterinary care, and safe handling.
LIFESPAN: Ferrets typically live 6–10 yrs.
DOMESTIC ROLE: Companion animal, pest control historically, and interactive household pet.
NOTABLE BREEDS / VARIETIES: Standard sable, albino, cinnamon, silver, and panda color patterns.
INTERESTING FACTS: Ferret kits sleep up to 18 hours a day during early development. They imprint strongly on caregivers. Domestic ferrets cannot survive independently in the wild. Ferret kits communicate early through soft chirps and squeaks before developing adult vocalizations. Their flexible spine permits a range of twisting and turning beyond that of most other mammals.

Ferret kit. Illustration copyright © Lochlainn Seabrook.

# FLEMISH GIANT RABBIT

COMMON NAME: Flemish Giant Rabbit.
BABY NAME: Kit.
SCIENTIFIC NAME: *Oryctolagus cuniculus domesticus*.
ANIMAL TYPE: Domestic mammal.
TAXONOMIC ORDER: Lagomorpha.
ORIGIN: Belgium, selectively bred in Flanders as a large-bodied domestic rabbit for fur, breeding, leather, meat, and exhibition.
DESCRIPTION: Flemish Giant kits are born small and fragile, with closed eyes and minimal fur despite their future massive size. Early growth is rapid, with noticeable weight gain occurring within the first few weeks. Kits develop long limbs and broad bodies early, hinting at the breed's eventual scale. Movement starts cautiously, with short hops that quickly become confident and powerful. As their eyes open, curiosity increases and exploration becomes constant. Muscle mass and bone thickness build steadily, requiring proper nutrition during early development. Kits mature physically faster than many smaller rabbit breeds but remain juvenile in behavior for several months. Their large size does not diminish their gentle demeanor, which is often apparent even at a young age. Handling tolerance typically develops early. Social awareness emerges quickly.
SIZE: Newborn kits weigh approx. 3–4 oz and may reach 10–15 lb by 6 mos of age.
APPEARANCE: Long upright ears, broad head, powerful hind legs, and a dense, sleek coat on an elongated, heavy-boned body.
TEMPERAMENT: Calm, docile, and friendly, often tolerant of handling and human interaction.
CARE REQUIREMENTS: Require spacious housing, high-fiber diet, constant hay access, grooming, and careful handling due to their large size.
LIFESPAN: Flemish Giant Rabbits typically live 5–8 yrs.
DOMESTIC ROLE: Companion animal, exhibition rabbit, and educational breed for responsible large-animal care.
NOTABLE BREEDS / VARIETIES: Sandy, fawn, light gray, steel gray, black, blue, and white varieties.
INTERESTING FACTS: Flemish Giant kits grow faster than most domestic rabbits. Adults are among the largest rabbit breeds in the world. Despite size, they are often nicknamed "gentle giants." Growth continues for more than a year, longer than smaller breeds. Their calm temperament made them popular for meat and fur. Large bone structure contributes significantly to overall weight. Adequate space and nutrition are essential during development.

Flemish Giant rabbit kit. Illustration copyright © Lochlainn Seabrook.

# FRENCH BULLDOG

COMMON NAME: French Bulldog.
BABY NAME: Puppy.
SCIENTIFIC NAME: *Canis lupus familiaris.*
ANIMAL TYPE: Domestic mammal.
TAXONOMIC ORDER: Carnivora.
ORIGIN: France, developed in the 19th Century as a small companion dog derived from toy bulldogs.
DESCRIPTION: French Bulldog puppies are compact, heavy-set, and broad-chested even at a very young age. Their bodies appear stout and muscular, with a low center of gravity and thick neck. Puppies move with a slightly rolling gait as coordination develops, giving them a charming, deliberate walk. The head is large in proportion to the body, with a short muzzle that defines the breed early. Facial expressions are highly animated, often giving puppies a curious or comical look. Social attachment forms quickly, and puppies strongly bond to human caretakers. Growth is steady rather than rapid, with bone and muscle filling out before height increases. Puppies are playful but not overly energetic, preferring short bursts of activity. Early training benefits from consistency and positive reinforcement. Sensitivity to heat may appear even in puppyhood due to brachycephalic structure. Vocal sounds such as snorting and grunting are common from an early age. Puppies often seek close physical contact and enjoy resting against people or littermates.
SIZE: Newborn puppies typically weigh 0.5–1 lb and reach 16–28 lb by adulthood.
APPEARANCE: Large upright bat ears, short flat muzzle, compact muscular body, and smooth short coat.
TEMPERAMENT: Affectionate, friendly, alert, and playful, with a calm disposition and strong people focus.
CARE REQUIREMENTS: Require climate control, careful feeding, moderate exercise, wrinkle cleaning, and gentle training.
LIFESPAN: French Bulldogs typically live 10–12 yrs.
DOMESTIC ROLE: Companion animal, household pet, and emotional support dog.
NOTABLE BREEDS / VARIETIES: Fawn, brindle, cream, pied, and various solid color patterns.
INTERESTING FACTS: French Bulldog puppies are born with soft ears that gradually stand upright. The breed cannot swim well due to body structure. They rose to popularity among Parisian working and artistic communities during the late 19th Century.

French Bulldog puppy. Illustration copyright © Lochlainn Seabrook.

# GOLDEN RETRIEVER

COMMON NAME: Golden Retriever.
BABY NAME: Puppy.
SCIENTIFIC NAME: *Canis lupus familiaris*.
ANIMAL TYPE: Domestic mammal.
TAXONOMIC ORDER: Carnivora.
ORIGIN: Scotland, developed as a gun dog for retrieving waterfowl and upland game.
DESCRIPTION: Golden Retriever puppies are soft-bodied, round-faced dogs with an immediately friendly expression. At birth they are sturdy but pliable, with rapid early growth that emphasizes balance rather than bulk. Puppies show strong human focus early, often following movement and responding quickly to voices. Their coordination develops steadily, allowing confident movement within weeks. Play behavior is frequent and gentle, with early signs of retrieving instincts such as carrying objects. Puppies display high learning capacity and strong memory retention. Social curiosity is pronounced, making them highly responsive to interaction. Energy levels are moderate but consistent, requiring structured play and rest. Coat texture begins soft and dense, thickening as the puppy matures. Physical development is even and proportional, producing a smooth transition into adolescence. Early emotional sensitivity allows puppies to bond quickly with caregivers. This strong attachment contributes to their reliability as working and companion dogs later in life.
SIZE: Newborn puppies typically weigh 1–1.5 lb and reach 30–50 lb by 6 mos of age.
APPEARANCE: Fluffy golden coat, dark round eyes, broad head, soft muzzle, and a sturdy, well-balanced frame.
TEMPERAMENT: Affectionate, intelligent, eager to please, and socially attentive with people and other animals.
CARE REQUIREMENTS: Require consistent feeding, early training, daily exercise, coat brushing, and regular social exposure.
LIFESPAN: Golden Retrievers typically live 10–12 yrs.
DOMESTIC ROLE: Family companion, service dog, therapy dog, hunting retriever, and obedience working dog.
NOTABLE BREEDS / VARIETIES: American Golden Retriever, British Golden Retriever, and Canadian Golden Retriever lines.
INTERESTING FACTS: Golden Retriever puppies instinctively carry objects without damaging them. The breed ranks among the most trainable dogs worldwide. Their friendly temperament remains stable from puppyhood into adulthood. Early selection emphasized soft mouth, patience, and cooperation with humans.

Golden retriever puppy. Illustration copyright © Lochlainn Seabrook.

# GOLDFISH

COMMON NAME: Goldfish.
BABY NAME: Fry.
SCIENTIFIC NAME: *Carassius auratus*.
ANIMAL TYPE: Domestic fish.
TAXONOMIC ORDER: Cypriniformes.
ORIGIN: East Asia, selectively bred from native wild carp in China over 1,000 yrs ago.
DESCRIPTION: Goldfish fry are tiny, translucent aquatic animals that emerge from eggs only a few days after spawning. At hatching, fry rely on a yolk sac for nourishment before beginning free swimming. Their early bodies are slender and dark, often appearing brown or gray rather than gold. Color development occurs gradually as pigments form during growth. Fry are highly sensitive to water quality and temperature changes in their earliest stages. Movement is quick and darting, driven by instinctive feeding and avoidance behaviors. As they mature, body shape begins to widen and fins become more defined. Selective breeding traits such as tail length or head growth do not appear immediately. Fry grow rapidly under proper conditions, requiring frequent feeding and clean water. Early survival depends heavily on stable environments and protection from larger fish. Development continues steadily over several mos until juvenile features are fully visible. During this period, growth rate and final coloration are strongly influenced by diet, space, and water quality. Consistent care during early life stages determines long-term health and form.
SIZE: Newly hatched fry measure about 0.2 in and may reach 1–2 in within several mos.
APPEARANCE: Slender body, transparent fins, dark early coloration, and undeveloped tail shape.
TEMPERAMENT: Non-aggressive, instinct-driven, and constantly active while feeding and exploring.
CARE REQUIREMENTS: Require clean, oxygenated water, gentle filtration, frequent feeding, and stable temps.
LIFESPAN: Goldfish typically live 10–20 yrs with proper care.
DOMESTIC ROLE: Ornamental aquarium fish and educational pet for observing growth and development.
NOTABLE BREEDS / VARIETIES: Common goldfish, Comet, Fantail, Ryukin, Oranda, and Telescope Eye.
INTERESTING FACTS: Goldfish fry are not born gold in color. Selective breeding determines adult shape and fin length. Goldfish can eventually recognize feeding routines and individual keepers.

Goldfish fry. Illustration copyright © Lochlainn Seabrook.

# GOOSE

COMMON NAME: Goose.
BABY NAME: Gosling.
SCIENTIFIC NAME: *Anser anser domesticus*.
ANIMAL TYPE: Domestic bird.
TAXONOMIC ORDER: Anseriformes.
ORIGIN: Eurasia, domesticated from wild gray geese for meat, eggs, feathers, and guarding.
DESCRIPTION: Goose goslings hatch covered in soft down and are immediately mobile, often walking within hours. They are round-bodied, long-necked chicks with oversized feet that give them a slightly clumsy appearance. Goslings grow rapidly, doubling in size within days under proper care. Early development focuses on leg strength, allowing them to follow adult geese closely. Social bonding occurs almost instantly, with goslings imprinting strongly on parents or caretakers. They are highly vocal from birth, using soft peeps to communicate location and comfort. Feeding behavior begins immediately, with goslings grazing alongside adults. Growth is steady and visible week by week as down feathers gradually give way to juvenile plumage. Their posture becomes more upright as the neck lengthens. By a few mos of age, goslings resemble smaller versions of adult geese. Development emphasizes coordination, awareness, and flock integration. Their early confidence around water allows supervised swimming at a young age. Vocal communication strengthens quickly as goslings learn flock calls and warning signals.
SIZE: Newly hatched goslings weigh about 3–4 oz and may reach 10–15 lb within 3–4 mos.
APPEARANCE: Soft yellow or gray down, long flexible neck, flat bill, and large webbed feet.
TEMPERAMENT: Curious, social, alert, and strongly bonded to flock members or caretakers.
CARE REQUIREMENTS: Require access to water, grazing space, protection from predators, and proper starter feed.
LIFESPAN: Domestic geese typically live 10–20 yrs.
DOMESTIC ROLE: Farm animal, natural weed control, feather and down production, meat, guard animal, and companion bird.
NOTABLE BREEDS / VARIETIES: Embden, Toulouse, Chinese, African, and Pilgrim geese.
INTERESTING FACTS: Goslings can recognize voices and faces early. They imprint within hours of hatching. Domestic geese have been used as farm guards for centuries due to their loud alarm calls.

Goose gosling. Illustration copyright © Lochlainn Seabrook.

# GUINEA PIG

COMMON NAME: Guinea Pig.
BABY NAME: Pup.
SCIENTIFIC NAME: *Cavia porcellus*.
ANIMAL TYPE: Domestic mammal.
TAXONOMIC ORDER: Rodentia.
ORIGIN: South America, domesticated from wild cavies by Indigenous peoples of the Andes for food and companionship.
DESCRIPTION: Guinea pig pups are born unusually well developed compared to many other small mammals. At birth, they have open eyes, fully formed teeth, and a dense coat of fur. Pups are mobile within hours and can walk, vocalize, and begin exploring their surroundings almost immediately. Unlike altricial rodents, guinea pig young do not rely entirely on nesting behavior. They nurse frequently but also sample solid foods within the first few days. Early development is rapid, with steady weight gain and increasing coordination. Pups display strong social instincts and stay close to the mother and littermates. Vocal communication begins early and includes soft squeaks used for contact. Growth is consistent rather than sudden, with body proportions remaining balanced. As they mature, pups quickly resemble miniature adults. Their early independence reflects their evolutionary history as prey animals. Despite this independence, maternal bonding remains important during early weeks.
SIZE: Newborn pups typically weigh 2–4 oz and reach 1–2 lb within several wks.
APPEARANCE: Compact body, rounded head, short legs, glossy fur, and bright open eyes from birth.
TEMPERAMENT: Calm, alert, and social, with gentle curiosity and frequent vocal communication.
CARE REQUIREMENTS: Require constant access to hay, clean bedding, warmth, and daily social interaction.
LIFESPAN: Guinea pigs typically live 5–7 yrs.
DOMESTIC ROLE: Small companion animal, educational pet, and social household mammal.
NOTABLE BREEDS / VARIETIES: American, Abyssinian, Peruvian, Silkie, and Teddy.
INTERESTING FACTS: Guinea pig pups are born with fur, teeth, and open eyes. Newborns can eat solid food within days. Pups begin learning social hierarchy behaviors within their first week. Guinea pigs are not pigs and are not from Guinea; they are rodents from South America that once sold for a "guinea" in Europe.

Guinea pig pup. Illustration copyright © Lochlainn Seabrook.

# HAMSTER

COMMON NAME: Hamster.
BABY NAME: Pup.
SCIENTIFIC NAME: *Mesocricetus auratus*.
ANIMAL TYPE: Domestic mammal.
TAXONOMIC ORDER: Rodentia.
ORIGIN: Western Asia, with modern domestic hamsters descended primarily from Syrian wild populations.
DESCRIPTION: Baby hamsters are born extremely small, hairless, and blind, relying entirely on the mother for warmth and nourishment. During the first week, pups grow rapidly, doubling in size and developing faint skin pigmentation. Fine fur begins to appear within days, followed by the opening of the ears and eyes as coordination improves. By two wks of age, pups begin exploring the nest and sampling solid food while still nursing. Movement shifts quickly from crawling to quick, darting motions typical of rodents. Development is fast compared to many mammals, with independence reached early. Hamster pups display strong instinctual behaviors, including burrowing and food hoarding, even before weaning. Growth continues steadily, with body proportions remaining compact and rounded. Early handling can influence tolerance of human interaction later in life. By 4–5 wks, pups resemble miniature adults. Social hierarchy behaviors may also emerge as littermates interact more frequently. Nest-cleaning and self-grooming behaviors begin to appear during this stage.
SIZE: Newborn pups weigh under 0.1 oz and reach 3–5 oz as adults.
APPEARANCE: Tiny rounded body, short limbs, developing fur, small ears, bead-like eyes, and expanding cheek pouches.
TEMPERAMENT: Curious, alert, and energetic, though young pups may be skittish until accustomed to handling.
CARE REQUIREMENTS: Require warmth, soft bedding, gradual weaning, quiet housing, and careful handling during early growth.
LIFESPAN: Hamsters typically live 2–3 yrs.
DOMESTIC ROLE: Small companion animal suited for observation, gentle handling, and educational pet keeping.
NOTABLE BREEDS / VARIETIES: Syrian, dwarf Campbell's, dwarf Winter White, and Roborovski hamsters.
INTERESTING FACTS: Hamster pups can develop cheek pouches before full weaning. Their teeth grow continuously from birth. Syrian hamsters were first domesticated from a single wild litter in the 1930s. Their closest living relatives are voles and lemmings.

Hamster pup. Illustration copyright © Lochlainn Seabrook.

# HEDGEHOG

COMMON NAME: Hedgehog.
BABY NAME: Hoglet.
SCIENTIFIC NAME: *Atelerix albiventris*.
ANIMAL TYPE: Domestic mammal.
TAXONOMIC ORDER: Eulipotyphla.
ORIGIN: Central and eastern Africa, later bred in captivity for companionship. Closest living relatives: gymnures, shrews, moles.
DESCRIPTION: Hedgehog hoglets are born extremely small and fragile, with eyes and ears sealed shut at birth. Their initial spines are soft and pale, emerging within hrs and hardening gradually over the first several days. Hoglets remain dependent on their mother for warmth, nutrition, and protection during early development. Within 2–3 wks, their eyes open and exploratory behavior begins. Movement transitions from clumsy crawling to cautious walking as coordination improves. Hoglets are naturally quiet and observant, often freezing when startled. As they mature, defensive curling behavior becomes more refined. Growth is steady, with body mass increasing rapidly during the first 6–8 wks. By weaning age, hoglets resemble miniature adults in structure. Early handling helps reduce stress and encourages tolerance of human interaction. Individual personality traits begin to appear during this stage, ranging from timid to mildly inquisitive. Activity levels increase noticeably at night as natural nocturnal instincts emerge. These behaviors signal the onset of independent juvenile development.
SIZE: Newborn hoglets weigh under 1 oz and reach 8–14 oz by 8–10 wks of age.
APPEARANCE: Small rounded body covered in short protective spines, pointed snout, dark eyes, and tiny rounded ears.
TEMPERAMENT: Shy, quiet, and alert, with a natural tendency toward cautious curiosity rather than overt affection.
CARE REQUIREMENTS: Require stable warmth, soft bedding, high-protein diet, gentle handling, and a quiet enclosure.
LIFESPAN: Hedgehogs typically live 4–6 yrs.
DOMESTIC ROLE: Exotic companion animal, educational pet, and small-scale hobby animal.
NOTABLE BREEDS / VARIETIES: Standard gray, albino, cinnamon, pinto, and snowflake color morphs.
INTERESTING FACTS: Hoglets are born with soft spines beneath the skin that emerge shortly after birth. Hedgehogs can run, climb, and swim despite their compact size. When threatened, they roll into a tight defensive ball using specialized muscles.

Hedgehog hoglet. Illustration copyright © Lochlainn Seabrook.

# HIGHLAND CATTLE

COMMON NAME: Highland Cattle.
BABY NAME: Calf.
SCIENTIFIC NAME: *Bos taurus*.
ANIMAL TYPE: Domestic mammal.
TAXONOMIC ORDER: Artiodactyla.
ORIGIN: Scottish Highlands, domesticated cattle selectively bred over centuries for rugged terrain, harsh weather, and sparse grazing conditions.
DESCRIPTION: Highland calves are born sturdy, compact, and well adapted to cold environments from the start. Their bodies are short and solid, with strong legs that allow them to stand and nurse soon after birth. Even as newborns, calves show an alert, steady demeanor rather than nervousness. Growth is gradual and well balanced, favoring strength and endurance over rapid size increase. Calves remain close to their mothers for protection and warmth, especially in cold or windy conditions. Early movement is confident, with a sure-footed gait suited to uneven ground. As they mature, muscle and bone density increase steadily, supporting long-term hardiness. Calves develop resilience early, tolerating weather conditions that challenge many other cattle breeds. Social awareness appears quickly, with calves recognizing herd structure and hierarchy. The breed's slow, deliberate growth results in long-lived, physically robust adults.
SIZE: Newborn calves typically weigh 50–75 lb and reach 250–350 lb by 6 mos of age.
APPEARANCE: Thick shaggy coat, compact body, short legs, broad head, and developing horns partially hidden by long hair.
TEMPERAMENT: Calm, gentle, and observant, with a quiet confidence and low reactivity when handled properly.
CARE REQUIREMENTS: Require access to pasture, shelter from extreme heat, regular veterinary care, and minimal grain supplementation.
LIFESPAN: Highland Cattle commonly live 15–20 yrs.
DOMESTIC ROLE: Beef production, conservation grazing, small farms, hides, leather, and heritage livestock preservation.
NOTABLE BREEDS / VARIETIES: Red, black, dun, yellow, brindle, and silver Highland color forms.
INTERESTING FACTS: Highland calves inherit one of the longest coats of any cattle breed. Their thick hair reduces the need for body fat insulation. The breed is among the oldest registered cattle breeds in the world. Long curved horns develop in both sexes and aid in foraging through snow and brush.

Highland cattle calf. Illustration copyright © Lochlainn Seabrook.

# HIMALAYAN CAT

COMMON NAME: Himalayan Cat.
BABY NAME: Kitten.
SCIENTIFIC NAME: *Felis catus*.
ANIMAL TYPE: Domestic mammal.
TAXONOMIC ORDER: Carnivora.
ORIGIN: United States and United Kingdom; developed in the mid-20$^{th}$ Century by crossbreeding Persian cats with Siamese cats to combine long coats with colorpoint markings.
DESCRIPTION: Himalayan kittens are compact, round-bodied babies with soft features and pronounced facial structure from birth. Their bodies are sturdy and low to the ground, with short legs supporting a broad chest. Kittens are born light in color, with darker colorpoints gradually developing on the ears, face, paws, and tail as they grow. Movement is gentle and deliberate rather than athletic or fast. Himalayan kittens tend to be calm and observant, spending long periods resting between short bursts of play. Their growth is steady, with the coat thickening significantly during the first year. Facial features become more defined over time, including the shortened nose and rounded head. Vocalization is usually soft and infrequent, reflecting their quiet nature. Kittens mature slowly compared to short-haired breeds. Early handling is important due to their long fur and facial structure.
SIZE: Newborn kittens weigh about 3–4 oz and reach 5–9 lb as adults.
APPEARANCE: Long dense coat, round head, short muzzle, large round eyes, and contrasting colorpoint markings.
TEMPERAMENT: Gentle, affectionate, and calm, with a preference for quiet environments and close human companionship.
CARE REQUIREMENTS: Require daily grooming, regular eye cleaning, indoor living, and careful monitoring of breathing and diet.
LIFESPAN: Himalayan cats typically live 12–15 yrs.
DOMESTIC ROLE: Indoor companion cat, lap cat, and low-activity household pet.
NOTABLE BREEDS / VARIETIES: Seal point, blue point, chocolate point, lilac point, flame point, and tortie point.
INTERESTING FACTS: Himalayan kittens are born nearly white before colorpoints appear. The breed is sometimes called Colorpoint Persian. Their eye color is always blue regardless of coat variation due to genetics and albinism.

Himalayan cat kitten. Illustration copyright © Lochlainn Seabrook.

# JERSEY CATTLE

COMMON NAME: Jersey Cattle.
BABY NAME: Calf.
SCIENTIFIC NAME: *Bos taurus*.
ANIMAL TYPE: Domestic mammal.
TAXONOMIC ORDER: Artiodactyla.
ORIGIN: Jersey Island in the English Channel, selectively bred for high-quality dairy production.
DESCRIPTION: Jersey calves are small, delicate-boned newborns known for their alert expressions and quick early development. At birth, calves are noticeably lighter and more refined than many other dairy breeds, which contributes to easier calving. Their growth during the first months is steady rather than rapid, emphasizing efficiency over bulk. Jersey calves often display early curiosity, standing and nursing quickly after birth. Muscle and skeletal development favors agility rather than mass. As they mature, calves retain a fine frame and smooth body lines. Early handling is common in dairy settings, making calves accustomed to human presence. Their metabolism develops efficiently, supporting the breed's reputation for feed conversion. Coat texture becomes sleeker with age, and physical proportions remain compact. The early form of the calf closely resembles the adult breed's refined silhouette. Overall growth emphasizes balance and long-term productivity rather than size alone. This refined build remains consistent into adulthood.
SIZE: Newborn calves typically weigh 40–55 lb and reach 250–350 lb by 6 mos of age.
APPEARANCE: Small head, large dark eyes, fine bone structure, short face, and a smooth fawn to light brown coat.
TEMPERAMENT: Calm, gentle, and alert, with a curious nature and strong responsiveness to handling.
CARE REQUIREMENTS: Require consistent feeding, clean housing, regular health monitoring, and early socialization.
LIFESPAN: Jersey cattle typically live 18–22 yrs.
DOMESTIC ROLE: Dairy production, small-scale farming, and efficient milk yield with high butterfat content.
NOTABLE BREEDS / VARIETIES: Standard Jersey cattle with color variations ranging from light fawn to dark brown.
INTERESTING FACTS: Jersey calves mature earlier than many dairy breeds. Their milk later produces some of the highest butterfat levels in the world. Jerseys are among the smallest common dairy cattle breeds and produce rich milk using less feed.

Jersey cattle calf. Illustration copyright © Lochlainn Seabrook.

# LLAMA

COMMON NAME: Llama.
BABY NAME: Cria.
SCIENTIFIC NAME: *Lama glama*.
ANIMAL TYPE: Domestic mammal.
TAXONOMIC ORDER: Artiodactyla.
ORIGIN: Andes Mountains of South America, domesticated by Indigenous peoples for fiber, transport, and companionship.
DESCRIPTION: Llama crias are long-legged, wide-eyed newborns that can stand and walk within an hr of birth. Their bodies are lightly built at first, with a soft skeletal frame that strengthens rapidly during the first few mos. Unlike many mammals, crias are born without a heavy fat layer, giving them a slender and delicate appearance. They rely on alertness, balance, and mobility rather than size for early survival. Growth is steady and proportional, with rapid leg development followed by gradual chest and muscle expansion. Cria behavior is calm and observant, often remaining close to the dam while cautiously exploring nearby space. Vocal communication begins early, with gentle humming used for reassurance and bonding. Their digestive system develops slowly, transitioning from milk to forage as the rumen matures. Coordination improves quickly, allowing confident movement across uneven terrain. By 6 mos, crias closely resemble adult llamas but retain a softer outline and finer facial features. Early curiosity encourages interaction with herd members and caretakers.
SIZE: Newborn crias weigh 20–35 lb and reach 150–200 lb by 6 mos of age.
APPEARANCE: Long neck, upright ears, large dark eyes, slim legs, and a soft woolly coat.
TEMPERAMENT: Gentle, curious, and alert, with a calm disposition and strong social bonding instincts.
CARE REQUIREMENTS: Require nursing, shelter from extreme weather, gradual weaning, parasite control, and gentle routine handling.
LIFESPAN: Llamas typically live 15–25 yrs.
DOMESTIC ROLE: Fiber production, pack animal, livestock guardian, therapy animal, and companion.
NOTABLE BREEDS / VARIETIES: Classic llama types selectively bred for fiber quality, packing strength, or show traits.
INTERESTING FACTS: Llama crias nurse almost exclusively while standing. They communicate primarily through humming. Most crias are born during daylight hrs for warmth and safety.

Llama cria. Illustration copyright © Lochlainn Seabrook.

# MAINE COON CAT

COMMON NAME: Maine Coon Cat.
BABY NAME: Kitten.
SCIENTIFIC NAME: *Felis catus*.
ANIMAL TYPE: Domestic mammal.
TAXONOMIC ORDER: Carnivora.
ORIGIN: United States, developed in New England as a hardy working cat adapted to cold climates.
DESCRIPTION: Maine Coon Cat kittens are large-boned, slow-maturing kittens known for their oversized paws, long bodies, and gentle demeanor from birth. Even as young kittens, they display notable size compared to most domestic breeds. Their growth rate is gradual, with full physical maturity often taking several yrs. Early development emphasizes strength, coordination, and balance rather than speed. Kittens are highly alert and observant, often following people from room to room. Play behavior tends to be deliberate and intelligent rather than frantic. Social bonding begins early, with kittens showing strong attachment to household members. Vocalization is present but soft, often expressed as chirps rather than meows. Physical proportions elongate steadily, with tail and ear size becoming especially prominent during juvenile stages. Their early structure already reflects the rectangular, muscular frame of the adult cat. Coat texture begins fluffy and becomes denser with age. Seasonal coat thickening may already be noticeable in cooler environments.
SIZE: Newborn kittens weigh about 3–5 oz and may reach 8–12 lb by 6 mos of age.
APPEARANCE: Large ears with tufting, bushy tail, broad chest, long shaggy coat, and oversized paws.
TEMPERAMENT: Gentle, affectionate, intelligent, and calm, with playful curiosity and strong human bonding.
CARE REQUIREMENTS: Require high-quality nutrition, regular grooming, social interaction, and room to move and climb.
LIFESPAN: Maine Coon Cats typically live 12–15 yrs.
DOMESTIC ROLE: Family companion, indoor cat, and interactive household pet.
NOTABLE BREEDS / VARIETIES: Natural color patterns including brown tabby, black, silver, red, and tortoiseshell.
INTERESTING FACTS: Maine Coon kittens are sometimes called "gentle giants" even at a young age. Their large paws help distribute weight on snow. The breed is one of the oldest native cat breeds in North America with documented colonial origins.

Maine Coon cat kitten. Illustration copyright © Lochlainn Seabrook.

# MINIATURE DONKEY

COMMON NAME: Miniature Donkey.
BABY NAME: Foal.
SCIENTIFIC NAME: *Equus africanus asinus*.
ANIMAL TYPE: Domestic mammal.
TAXONOMIC ORDER: Perissodactyla.
ORIGIN: Mediterranean regions, refined in the U.S. as a small companion and working donkey breed.
DESCRIPTION: Miniature donkey foals are compact, soft-coated, and long-limbed at birth, with proportions that appear slightly oversized for their small bodies. Their ears are already prominent and upright, contributing to their instantly recognizable appearance. Foals are cautious but curious, often staying close to their dam during early days. Movement is deliberate and careful, with a naturally steady gait rather than quick bursts of speed. Growth is slow and controlled, allowing strong bones and joints to develop evenly. Miniature donkey foals are highly observant and learn routines quickly through repetition. Early social bonding with humans is common and long-lasting. They display early vocalization, using soft brays to communicate with herd members. Foals mature mentally at a measured pace, remaining juvenile in behavior longer than many livestock species. Their early development emphasizes stability, awareness, and powerful social attachment. Young foals show strong herd awareness and can recognize familiar humans within weeks of birth. They also demonstrate early problem-solving skills, especially when navigating enclosures or following established paths.
SIZE: Newborn foals typically weigh 15–25 lb and stand 18–22 in. tall at birth.
APPEARANCE: Long ears, short muzzle, thick neck, straight legs, and a fluffy coat that may darken or lighten with age.
TEMPERAMENT: Calm, gentle, intelligent, and cautious, with strong bonding tendencies and a patient nature.
CARE REQUIREMENTS: Require regular feeding, hoof trimming, shelter, parasite control, and gentle handling.
LIFESPAN: Miniature donkeys commonly live 25–35 yrs.
DOMESTIC ROLE: Companion animal, pasture guardian, light farm work, and educational or therapy animal.
NOTABLE BREEDS / VARIETIES: Mediterranean Miniature Donkey and American Miniature Donkey lines.
INTERESTING FACTS: Miniature donkey foals are naturally quiet compared to horses. Their large ears help regulate body temperature. They are known for excellent long-term memory.

Miniature donkey foal. Illustration copyright © Lochlainn Seabrook.

# MINIATURE HORSE

COMMON NAME: Miniature Horse.
BABY NAME: Foal.
SCIENTIFIC NAME: *Equus ferus caballus*.
ANIMAL TYPE: Domestic mammal.
TAXONOMIC ORDER: Perissodactyla.
ORIGIN: Europe and North America, selectively bred from small horse stock for size, refinement, and temperament.
DESCRIPTION: Miniature horse foals are proportionally built at birth, resembling full-sized horses in near-perfect miniature form. Their legs are long relative to body size, giving them a delicate but balanced appearance. Foals are alert and mobile within hours, quickly learning to follow the mare. Movement is light, energetic, and coordinated, reflecting strong musculoskeletal development. Growth is steady rather than rapid, with careful breeding emphasizing sound structure over extreme size reduction. Miniature horse foals are highly social and responsive to human presence early on. They display strong curiosity, often investigating new environments with confidence. Early training and handling shape calm, adaptable behavior. Their mental development is quick, allowing foals to recognize routines and handlers at a young age. Juvenile play behavior includes short runs, hops, and mock sparring with other foals. Early exercise supports proper joint alignment and long-term soundness. Foals also develop strong spatial awareness, allowing them to navigate obstacles with surprising precision.
SIZE: Newborn foals typically weigh 20–40 lb and stand 18–22 in. tall at birth.
APPEARANCE: Refined head, large eyes, straight legs, short back, and a smooth coat with balanced proportions.
TEMPERAMENT: Friendly, intelligent, gentle, and eager to interact, with a calm and cooperative disposition.
CARE REQUIREMENTS: Require regular feeding, hoof trimming, shelter, grooming, and early training to prevent obesity.
LIFESPAN: Miniature horses commonly live 25–35 yrs.
DOMESTIC ROLE: Companion animal, therapy work, driving, education, and exhibition.
NOTABLE BREEDS / VARIETIES: American Miniature Horse and European Miniature Horse bloodlines.
INTERESTING FACTS: Miniature horses are true horses, not ponies. Foals mature mentally faster than many large breeds. Worldwide they are often used in hospitals and schools as therapy animals due to their size and temperament.

Miniature horse foal. Illustration copyright © Lochlainn Seabrook.

# MINI LOP RABBIT

COMMON NAME: Mini Lop Rabbit.
BABY NAME: Kit.
SCIENTIFIC NAME: *Oryctolagus cuniculus.*
ANIMAL TYPE: Domestic mammal.
TAXONOMIC ORDER: Lagomorpha.
ORIGIN: Germany, developed in the $20^{th}$ Century as a smaller lop-eared companion rabbit.
DESCRIPTION: Mini Lop kits are compact, round-bodied baby rabbits with soft proportions and noticeably oversized heads. At birth they are tiny, fragile, and lightly furred, with ears that initially sit upright before gradually lopping as they mature. Growth during the first few weeks is rapid, with weight gain occurring faster than limb elongation. Kits spend most of their early days nursing, sleeping, and huddling for warmth. As their eyes open, movement becomes more coordinated, though still clumsy and gentle. Mini Lop kits begin exploring their surroundings earlier than many larger rabbit breeds. Their bodies remain dense and muscular rather than elongated as they grow. By weaning age, the breed's signature rounded shape is already evident. Mental development is quick, with kits learning routines and recognizing caregivers early. Their juvenile appearance closely resembles a scaled-down adult rather than a lanky adolescent form.
SIZE: Newborn kits weigh approx. 1–2 oz and reach 2–3 lb by 4–5 mos of age.
APPEARANCE: Short rounded body, thick neck, plush dense fur, broad head, and ears that hang down close to the cheeks.
TEMPERAMENT: Calm, affectionate, curious, and social, with a gentle disposition well suited to handling.
CARE REQUIREMENTS: Require warm nesting, gradual weaning, high-quality hay, fresh water, gentle handling, and clean living space.
LIFESPAN: Mini Lop Rabbits typically live 7–10 yrs.
DOMESTIC ROLE: Companion animal, pet rabbit, and popular breed for families and rabbit exhibitions.
NOTABLE BREEDS / VARIETIES: Broken pattern, solid colors, tortoiseshell, and shaded coat varieties.
NTERESTING FACTS: Mini Lop kits are born with upright ears that slowly drop over time. The breed is one of the most popular pet rabbits worldwide. Their dense body type gives them a heavier feel than expected for their size. Kits can recognize familiar human voices within their first few weeks of life.

Mini lop rabbit kit. Illustration copyright © Lochlainn Seabrook.

# MULE

COMMON NAME: Mule.
BABY NAME: Foal.
SCIENTIFIC NAME: *Equus asinus* × *Equus ferus caballus*.
ANIMAL TYPE: Domestic mammal.
TAXONOMIC ORDER: Perissodactyla.
ORIGIN: Worldwide, hybrid developed through the deliberate breeding of a donkey and a horse to combine strength, endurance, and intelligence.
DESCRIPTION: Mule foals are sturdy, long-legged youngsters that show a blend of donkey and horse traits from birth. Their bodies are typically more compact than horse foals, with strong joints and dense bone structure that supports future load-bearing work. Movement is confident and balanced, often showing surprising coordination at an early age. Mule foals tend to be alert and observant, carefully assessing new environments before acting. Growth is steady rather than rapid, allowing muscles and tendons to develop evenly. Their hybrid genetics often result in increased resilience and physical efficiency. Social bonding occurs early, especially with the mother and human handlers. Foals learn quickly through observation and repetition, showing strong memory retention even at a young age. As they mature, their proportions lengthen, and strength becomes more apparent. Early handling helps reinforce trust, calm behavior, and long-term reliability. Many foals display a thoughtful, deliberate approach to movement rather than impulsive behavior. This cautious confidence often contributes to the mule's reputation for dependability later in life.
APPEARANCE: Long ears, straight legs, narrow hooves, short mane, and a body combining horse height with donkey sturdiness.
TEMPERAMENT: Intelligent, cautious, steady-natured, and affectionate, with a strong sense of self-preservation.
CARE REQUIREMENTS: Require proper nutrition, hoof care, social interaction, shelter, and gentle consistent training.
LIFESPAN: Mules commonly live 30–40 yrs.
DOMESTIC ROLE: Pack animal, farm worker, trail mount, and reliable companion animal.
NOTABLE BREEDS / VARIETIES: Draft mule, saddle mule, pack mule, and miniature mule.
INTERESTING FACTS: Most mules are sterile due to mismatched chromosomes. Mule foals inherit endurance from donkeys and size from horses. Mules are known for exceptional problem-solving ability, often showing strong independent judgment.

Mule foal. Illustration copyright © Lochlainn Seabrook.

# NORWEGIAN FOREST CAT

COMMON NAME: Norwegian Forest Cat.
BABY NAME: Kitten.
SCIENTIFIC NAME: *Felis catus*.
ANIMAL TYPE: Domestic mammal.
TAXONOMIC ORDER: Carnivora.
ORIGIN: Norway, developed naturally as a cold-climate farm and forest cat adapted to harsh Scandinavian winters.
DESCRIPTION: Norwegian Forest Cat kittens are large-boned, sturdy babies with dense coats that develop rapidly even in early weeks. From birth, kittens show strong climbing instincts and excellent balance, reflecting their forest-dwelling ancestry. Their growth is slower than many domestic cats, with full physical maturity reached later than average. Kittens are agile and alert, often exploring vertical spaces as soon as coordination allows. Muscular development is gradual, supporting powerful hind legs and a long, flexible body. Early play behavior emphasizes climbing, leaping, and stalking rather than short bursts of speed. The thick undercoat begins forming early, offering insulation against cold and damp conditions. Facial features are soft at first but gradually sharpen into the breed's characteristic triangular head shape. Kittens bond closely with caretakers while maintaining an independent streak. Mental development is steady, producing a confident but calm young cat suited to both activity and rest. Their steady temperament makes them well adapted to structured indoor environments.
SIZE: Newborn kittens typically weigh 3–4 oz and reach 6–10 lb by 6 mos of age.
APPEARANCE: Semi-long thick coat, bushy tail, tufted ears, almond-shaped eyes, and a strong, athletic frame.
TEMPERAMENT: Calm, gentle, and intelligent, with playful curiosity and an independent but affectionate nature.
CARE REQUIREMENTS: Require regular grooming, balanced nutrition, climbing enrichment, and routine veterinary care.
LIFESPAN: Norwegian Forest Cats typically live 12–16 yrs.
DOMESTIC ROLE: Family companion, indoor climber, and adaptable household cat well suited to cooler climates.
NOTABLE BREEDS / VARIETIES: Classic brown tabby, black, white, blue, cream, and various bicolor patterns.
INTERESTING FACTS: Norwegian Forest Cat kittens mature more slowly than most breeds. Their coats are naturally water-resistant. The breed is featured in Scandinavian folklore as a magical forest cat associated with strength and endurance.

Norwegian forest cat kitten. Illustration copyright © Lochlainn Seabrook.

# ORPINGTON CHICKEN

COMMON NAME: Orpington chicken.
BABY NAME: Chick.
SCIENTIFIC NAME: *Gallus gallus domesticus*.
ANIMAL TYPE: Domestic bird.
TAXONOMIC ORDER: Galliformes.
ORIGIN: England, developed in the late 19$^{th}$ Century as a hardy, dual-purpose poultry breed suited to cool climates.
DESCRIPTION: Orpington chicks hatch as round, downy babies with notably soft, plush feathering even in the earliest days. Their bodies appear compact and well-padded, giving them a teddy bear–like look compared to many other chicken breeds. Growth is steady and balanced, with strong legs developing early to support their broad frame. Chicks are typically calm and unhurried in movement, preferring to explore slowly rather than dart about nervously. Their early temperament reflects the breed's long history of selective breeding for gentleness and reliability. Feather development begins evenly across the body, creating a smooth transition from fluff to juvenile plumage. Orpington chicks adapt well to brooder environments and show strong cold tolerance as feathers come in. Social behavior emerges early, with chicks often staying close together. Vocalizations are soft and infrequent, indicating a generally relaxed disposition. By several wks of age, their rounded form becomes more pronounced.
SIZE: Chicks weigh about 1.5 oz at hatch and reach 3–4 lb by 4–5 mos of age.
APPEARANCE: Round body, fluffy down, short beak, sturdy legs, and a soft, full silhouette even when young.
TEMPERAMENT: Calm, friendly, and docile, with low aggression and strong tolerance of handling.
CARE REQUIREMENTS: Require warm brooder conditions, clean bedding, starter feed, fresh water, and gradual temperature reduction.
LIFESPAN: Orpington chickens typically live 6–10 yrs.
DOMESTIC ROLE: Egg production, meat bird, exhibition poultry, and gentle backyard companion.
NOTABLE BREEDS / VARIETIES: Buff, black, blue, white, and chocolate Orpington varieties.
INTERESTING FACTS: Orpington chicks feather more slowly than most breeds. Their rounded shape is intentional, bred for both productivity and appearance. Orpingtons were once considered Britain's ideal utility chicken. The breed quickly gained popularity for its calm temperament and dependable growth.

Orpington chicken chick. Illustration copyright © Lochlainn Seabrook.

# PARAKEET

COMMON NAME: Parakeet.
BABY NAME: Chick.
SCIENTIFIC NAME: *Melopsittacus undulatus*.
ANIMAL TYPE: Domestic bird.
TAXONOMIC ORDER: Psittaciformes.
ORIGIN: Australia, where wild parakeets evolved as nomadic flock birds adapted to open grasslands and semi-arid regions.
DESCRIPTION: Parakeet chicks hatch blind, featherless, and entirely dependent on parental care within the nest cavity. In the first days of life, growth is rapid, with soft down beginning to appear within a week. As feathers emerge, chicks quickly develop the compact body shape typical of the species. Wing feathers lengthen early, preparing the young bird for fledging. By several weeks of age, chicks become alert, vocal, and increasingly curious about their surroundings. Their coordination improves quickly as balance and grip strength develop. Juvenile parakeets show early social awareness and respond to movement and sound around the nest. Feeding transitions gradually from crop-fed regurgitated food to softened seeds. By the time fledging occurs, chicks resemble smaller, duller versions of adults. Early handling during this stage helps shape confidence and adaptability in domestic settings. Color mutations often become more visible as juvenile feathers replace early down.
SIZE: Newly hatched chicks weigh under 0.1 lb and reach 0.07–0.09 lb by fledging.
APPEARANCE: Small streamlined body, developing wing feathers, short tail at first, and dark eyes that lighten with age.
TEMPERAMENT: Curious, social, gentle, and highly responsive to interaction when properly socialized.
CARE REQUIREMENTS: Require warm nesting conditions, frequent feeding, clean housing, proper perches, and gradual introduction to solid food.
LIFESPAN: Parakeets typically live 7–15 yrs.
DOMESTIC ROLE: Companion bird, aviary species, and popular beginner pet known for vocalization and interaction.
NOTABLE BREEDS / VARIETIES: Standard green, blue, albino, lutino, pied, and spangle color mutations.
INTERESTING FACTS: Parakeet chicks develop faster than many parrots. Their beaks are strong enough to crack seeds before full maturity. Parakeets can begin mimicking sounds shortly after fledging. Early on chicks recognize parental calls.

Parakeet chick. Illustration copyright © Lochlainn Seabrook.

# PEKING DUCK

COMMON NAME: Peking Duck.
BABY NAME: Duckling.
SCIENTIFIC NAME: *Anas platyrhynchos domesticus.*
ANIMAL TYPE: Domestic bird.
TAXONOMIC ORDER: Anseriformes.
ORIGIN: China, selectively bred for centuries as a meat and utility duck known for rapid growth and calm disposition.
DESCRIPTION: Peking Duck ducklings hatch covered in soft yellow down and grow at an exceptionally fast rate compared to most domestic birds. Their bodies are round and compact from an early age, with strong legs that support steady walking within days of hatching. Ducklings are highly active and vocal, often moving together in tight groups for security. Feeding behavior begins immediately, with constant pecking and dabbling motions that encourage rapid weight gain. Growth is most intense during the first 8 wks, when body mass increases dramatically. Feathers begin replacing down within the first month, especially along the wings and back. Ducklings show early social bonding with caretakers when handled gently. Their posture becomes more upright as they mature, reflecting the breed's characteristic carriage. By adolescence, their body shape already resembles the adult form. Development prioritizes mass and strength rather than agility or flight.
SIZE: Newly hatched ducklings weigh about 2–3 oz and may reach 7–9 lb by 8–10 wks of age.
APPEARANCE: Yellow down as hatchlings, broad body, short neck, orange bill and feet; white feathers emerge as they grow.
TEMPERAMENT: Calm, friendly, and social, with low aggression and strong flocking behavior.
CARE REQUIREMENTS: Require clean water access, high-protein starter feed, warmth during early weeks, and protection from predators.
LIFESPAN: Peking Ducks typically live 8–12 yrs.
DOMESTIC ROLE: Meat production, small farm utility bird, feather, down, exhibition duck, and backyard companion.
NOTABLE BREEDS / VARIETIES: American Pekin, Jumbo Pekin, and exhibition lines.
INTERESTING FACTS: Peking ducklings can double their weight in just a few days. The breed cannot fly as adults due to body mass. Peking Ducks are one of the most widely raised domestic ducks in the world, valued for rapid growth and meat production.

Peking duck duckling. Illustration copyright © Lochlainn Seabrook.

# PERSIAN CAT

COMMON NAME: Persian Cat.
BABY NAME: Kitten.
SCIENTIFIC NAME: *Felis catus*.
ANIMAL TYPE: Domestic mammal.
TAXONOMIC ORDER: Carnivora.
ORIGIN: Ancient Persia (modern-day Iran), selectively refined over centuries for coat length and facial structure.
DESCRIPTION: Persian kittens are round-bodied, slow-moving, and notably plush from birth. Their development emphasizes softness and mass rather than agility, giving them a dense, teddy-bear appearance early on. Kittens grow steadily, with bone and muscle forming beneath an exceptionally thick coat. Facial structure develops gradually, with the short muzzle becoming more pronounced over time. Movement is calm and measured, even in youth, reflecting the breed's naturally low-energy disposition. Persian kittens spend long periods resting between brief play sessions. They show early attachment to familiar people and environments. Vocalization is minimal and soft. Coordination develops more slowly than in athletic cat breeds. Their growth favors fullness and symmetry rather than speed or leanness. By adolescence, their overall form closely resembles the adult cat.
SIZE: Newborn kittens weigh about 3–4 oz and reach 7–12 lb as adults.
APPEARANCE: Long flowing coat, compact body, short legs, rounded head, small ears, and large copper or blue eyes.
TEMPERAMENT: Calm, gentle, and affectionate, preferring quiet environments and predictable routines.
CARE REQUIREMENTS: Require daily grooming, eye cleaning, regular feeding, and indoor housing to protect the coat and health.
LIFESPAN: Persian Cats typically live 12–16 yrs.
DOMESTIC ROLE: Indoor companion cat valued for temperament, appearance, and low activity level.
NOTABLE BREEDS / VARIETIES: Doll Face Persian, Peke-Face Persian, solid, shaded, smoke, tabby, and colorpoint varieties.
INTERESTING FACTS: Persian kittens are born with shorter coats that lengthen over the first yr. The breed's flat facial structure requires extra eye care. Persians are among the oldest recognized cat breeds in the world. Persian kittens often retain a rounded, juvenile appearance well into adulthood, its calm demeanor making it one of the least vocal domestic cats. Persian kittens often do not develop a full adult coat until about 2 yrs of age.

Persian cat kitten. Illustration copyright © Lochlainn Seabrook.

# PIG

COMMON NAME: Pig.
BABY NAME: Piglet.
SCIENTIFIC NAME: *Sus scrofa domesticus*.
ANIMAL TYPE: Domestic mammal.
TAXONOMIC ORDER: Artiodactyla.
ORIGIN: Eurasia, domesticated from wild boar for meat, labor, and later companionship.
DESCRIPTION: Piglets are compact, round-bodied newborns with soft skin and short legs that support rapid early growth. At birth they are highly vocal and active, relying on strong instincts to nurse and compete for warmth. Their development is fast, with noticeable increases in weight and coordination within the first few weeks. Piglets quickly learn routines and respond to human handling, showing early signs of intelligence and social awareness. They are born with a strong rooting reflex and spend much of their time exploring surfaces with their snouts. Muscles and bone structure develop quickly to support steady weight gain. Piglets are sensitive to temperature and require warmth during early life. As they grow, their movements become more confident and purposeful. Curiosity dominates behavior, driving constant investigation of their surroundings. Early social exposure strongly shapes temperament and adaptability.
SIZE: Newborn piglets weigh about 2–3 lb and reach 20–35 lb by 8 wks of age.
APPEARANCE: Short legs, rounded body, smooth or lightly bristled skin, and a blunt snout with alert eyes.
TEMPERAMENT: Curious, intelligent, social, and responsive, with strong food motivation and playfulness.
CARE REQUIREMENTS: Need warmth, frequent feeding, clean bedding, social interaction, and secure containment.
LIFESPAN: Domestic pigs typically live 12–20 yrs.
DOMESTIC ROLE: Livestock animal, meat production, companion animal, and educational and petting farm animal.
NOTABLE BREEDS / VARIETIES: Yorkshire, Hampshire, Duroc, Berkshire, and miniature pot-bellied pigs.
INTERESTING FACTS: Piglets can recognize human voices within days of birth. They learn simple tasks faster than most mammals. Their snouts contain thousands of touch-sensitive receptors. Piglets communicate with littermates using distinct vocal calls. They begin social play behaviors within the first week of life. Newborn piglets are capable of running within hours of birth.

Pig piglet. Illustration copyright © Lochlainn Seabrook.

# PYGMY GOAT

COMMON NAME: Pygmy goat.
BABY NAME: Kid.
SCIENTIFIC NAME: *Capra aegagrus hircus*.
ANIMAL TYPE: Domestic mammal.
TAXONOMIC ORDER: Artiodactyla.
ORIGIN: West Africa, developed as a small, hardy goat breed adapted to tropical environments.
DESCRIPTION: Pygmy goat kids are compact, short-legged newborns with sturdy builds and rapid early development. They are born alert and agile, standing and nursing within minutes to hours after birth. Their small size does not limit activity, and kids are highly energetic from the start. Growth during the first weeks is steady, with strong muscle tone developing early. Kids display pronounced curiosity and quickly explore their surroundings. Social bonding begins immediately with the dam and herd members. Their coordination improves rapidly, allowing jumping and climbing behaviors at a very young age. Vocal communication is frequent and expressive. Early handling promotes calm, confident behavior. Pygmy goat kids are resilient and adapt well to varied environments. Their early development supports long-term hardiness and adaptability.
SIZE: Newborn kids weigh about 2–4 lb and reach 15–25 lb by 8 wks of age.
APPEARANCE: Short, stocky body, straight profile, upright ears, short legs, and a dense coat in varied colors.
TEMPERAMENT: Playful, alert, social, and confident, with strong curiosity and herd awareness.
CARE REQUIREMENTS: Require shelter, dry bedding, regular feeding, social interaction, hoof care, and secure fencing.
LIFESPAN: Pygmy goats typically live 10–15 yrs.
DOMESTIC ROLE: Livestock animal, companion animal, milk production, weed control, and educational or hobby farm animal.
NOTABLE BREEDS / VARIETIES: American Pygmy goat, African Pygmy goat.
INTERESTING FACTS: Pygmy goat kids are capable of jumping within their first days of life. They retain a compact size into adulthood. Their small stature makes them popular in petting farms and educational settings. Kids develop strong herd bonds early. They are known for climbing behavior disproportionate to their size. Pygmy goat kids use playful head-butting and hopping as early social learning behaviors within close-knit herd groups.

Pygmy goat kid. Illustration copyright © Lochlainn Seabrook.

# QUAIL

COMMON NAME: Quail.
BABY NAME: Chick.
SCIENTIFIC NAME: *Coturnix japonica*.
ANIMAL TYPE: Domestic bird.
TAXONOMIC ORDER: Galliformes.
ORIGIN: East Asia, domesticated primarily from Japanese quail for eggs, meat, and research use.
DESCRIPTION: Quail chicks are extremely small, round-bodied hatchlings covered in soft, downy feathers. They hatch fully mobile and alert, capable of walking and pecking within hours. Early growth is rapid, with noticeable increases in size and coordination during the first week. Chicks rely on instinctive feeding behaviors and quickly learn to follow movement and sound. Their metabolism is fast, requiring frequent access to food and warmth. Social grouping is important from the start, as chicks thrive in close proximity to others. Vocalizations are high-pitched and frequent during early life. Feather patterning begins to emerge within days. Muscular development supports quick bursts of movement. Early environmental stability strongly influences survival and temperament.
SIZE: Newly hatched chicks weigh about 0.2–0.3 oz and reach 3–5 oz by 4–5 wks of age.
APPEARANCE: Tiny, round body, short legs, large dark eyes, and striped or mottled down in tan, brown, or cream tones.
TEMPERAMENT: Alert, active, cautious, and social, with quick reflexes and strong flock awareness.
CARE REQUIREMENTS: Require consistent warmth, finely ground feed, shallow water access, clean bedding, and protection from drafts.
LIFESPAN: Domestic quail typically live 2–5 yrs.
DOMESTIC ROLE: Egg-laying bird, meat bird, laboratory species, and educational or hobby farm animal.
NOTABLE BREEDS / VARIETIES: Japanese quail, Jumbo Coturnix, English white, and tuxedo quail.
INTERESTING FACTS: Quail chicks grow faster than most domestic birds. They can begin short fluttering movements within days. Their rapid maturity allows egg production by 6–8 wks of age. Chicks imprint quickly on their environment. Despite their small size, they are highly efficient egg layers. Quail chicks rely on camouflage patterning even at hatch to reduce detection by predators, a key survival adaptation in the wild.

Quail chick. Illustration copyright © Lochlainn Seabrook.

# RAGDOLL CAT

COMMON NAME: Ragdoll cat.
BABY NAME: Kitten.
SCIENTIFIC NAME: *Felis catus*.
ANIMAL TYPE: Domestic mammal.
TAXONOMIC ORDER: Carnivora.
ORIGIN: United States, selectively bred in the 20$^{th}$ Century for gentle temperament and distinctive coat traits.
DESCRIPTION: Ragdoll kittens are born small, soft-bodied, and entirely dependent, with closed eyes and pale coats that gradually develop color. Early growth is steady, with rapid increases in coordination, strength, and awareness during the first weeks. They are notably relaxed when handled, often going limp in human arms even as young kittens. Social bonding begins early, with strong attachment to caregivers and littermates. Ragdoll kittens mature more slowly than many breeds, remaining physically and behaviorally juvenile for an extended period. Their early development emphasizes trust, calmness, and close human interaction. Muscle tone and skeletal size increase gradually, supporting their large adult frame. Sensory awareness sharpens quickly as vision and hearing develop. Play behavior is gentle rather than rough, reflecting the breed's placid nature. Early handling strongly reinforces their characteristic docility.
SIZE: Newborn kittens weigh about 3–4 oz and reach 2–4 lb by 8–10 wks of age.
APPEARANCE: Soft semi-long fur, rounded face, blue eyes, pale body coloration with darker points, and plush tail.
TEMPERAMENT: Gentle, affectionate, calm, and trusting, with low aggression and strong human bonding.
CARE REQUIREMENTS: Require warmth, regular feeding, gentle handling, litter training, grooming acclimation, and social interaction.
LIFESPAN: Ragdoll cats typically live 12–17 yrs.
DOMESTIC ROLE: Companion animal valued for temperament, appearance, and indoor suitability.
NOTABLE BREEDS / VARIETIES: Colorpoint, mitted, bicolor, lynx, and tortie patterns within the Ragdoll breed.
INTERESTING FACTS: Kittens are born white and develop color over several weeks. The breed is always blue-eyed, a defining trait present from kittenhood. Their relaxed response to handling appears very early. They are slower to reach full adult size than most cats. Ragdolls often follow their owners from room to room.

Ragdoll cat kitten. Illustration copyright © Lochlainn Seabrook.

# SHEEP

COMMON NAME: Sheep.
BABY NAME: Lamb.
SCIENTIFIC NAME: *Ovis aries*.
ANIMAL TYPE: Domestic mammal.
TAXONOMIC ORDER: Artiodactyla.
ORIGIN: Western Asia and the Middle East, domesticated from wild mouflon for wool, meat, milk, and hides.
DESCRIPTION: Lambs are small, long-legged newborns adapted for rapid mobility shortly after birth. They are precocial, standing and nursing within minutes to hours. Early life is focused on bonding with the ewe, feeding, and thermoregulation. Growth during the first weeks is steady and visibly rapid. Lambs are alert and responsive, quickly learning flock cues and following behavior. Their digestive system develops to transition from milk to grazing. Social awareness emerges early, with lambs recognizing their mothers by voice and scent. Muscular development supports increasing agility and short bursts of speed. Play behavior appears early and aids coordination. Lambs remain close to the flock for protection and security. Environmental exposure strongly influences resilience and health outcomes.
SIZE: Newborn lambs weigh about 5–12 lb and reach 40–70 lb by 3–4 mos of age.
APPEARANCE: Slender legs, compact body, soft woolly coat, narrow face, and large alert eyes.
TEMPERAMENT: Gentle, social, alert, and cautious, with strong flocking instincts.
CARE REQUIREMENTS: Require colostrum at birth, shelter from cold and wet conditions, regular feeding, clean bedding, and predator protection.
LIFESPAN: Domestic sheep typically live 10–12 yrs.
DOMESTIC ROLE: Livestock animal for wool, meat, milk, land management, and educational settings.
NOTABLE BREEDS / VARIETIES: Merino, Suffolk, Dorset, Hampshire, and Jacob.
INTERESTING FACTS: Lambs can recognize their mothers within hours of birth. They can remember dozens of individual faces. Lambs engage in play that improves balance and strength. Their wool fibers begin developing shortly after birth. Lambs use vocalizations to maintain contact with the ewe. They can follow flock movement patterns instinctively. Lambs often form strong social bonds with peers during early development.

Sheep lamb. Illustration copyright © Lochlainn Seabrook.

# SHETLAND PONY

COMMON NAME: Shetland pony.
BABY NAME: Foal.
SCIENTIFIC NAME: *Equus ferus caballus.*
ANIMAL TYPE: Domestic mammal.
TAXONOMIC ORDER: Perissodactyla.
ORIGIN: Shetland Islands of Scotland, developed through centuries of isolation, harsh climate, and selective breeding for strength and endurance.
DESCRIPTION: Shetland pony foals are small, compact, and sturdy at birth, built for survival in cold, windy environments. They stand quickly and nurse within hours, showing strong early coordination and balance. Dense bone structure and a low center of gravity are present from birth, supporting stability on uneven ground. Foals grow steadily rather than rapidly, developing muscle and strength before height. Their early behavior is alert but cautious, shaped by instinctive awareness of surroundings. The breed's hardiness is evident early, with foals tolerating cool temperatures better than many horse breeds. Movement is confident and efficient, favoring short, powerful strides. Social bonding with the dam is strong, and foals closely mirror adult herd behavior. Early handling helps shape calm, cooperative adults. Their growth pattern reflects the breed's long-term adaptation to limited resources.
SIZE: Newborn foals weigh about 20–30 lb and stand around 20–24 in. tall at birth.
APPEARANCE: Thick neck, short legs, rounded body, dense coat, small ears, and a broad, expressive face.
TEMPERAMENT: Calm, intelligent, independent, and strong-willed, with a steady and observant nature.
CARE REQUIREMENTS: Require regular grooming, hoof care, controlled feeding, shelter from heat, and consistent handling.
LIFESPAN: Shetland ponies often live 25–30 yrs.
DOMESTIC ROLE: Companion animal, children's riding pony, driving pony, educational animal, therapy animal.
NOTABLE BREEDS / VARIETIES: Standard Shetland, Miniature Shetland, and American Shetland Pony.
INTERESTING FACTS: Shetland foals are born with extremely dense bones relative to size. The breed was once used in coal mines due to strength and small stature. They require less food than larger horses. Foals develop thick winter coats early. Worldwide, Shetlands are among the longest-lived pony breeds on record.

Shetland pony foal. Illustration copyright © Lochlainn Seabrook.

# SILKIE CHICKEN

OMMON NAME: Silkie chicken.
BABY NAME: Chick.
SCIENTIFIC NAME: *Gallus gallus domesticus*.
ANIMAL TYPE: Domestic bird.
TAXONOMIC ORDER: Galliformes.
ORIGIN: China, selectively bred for ornamental traits, gentle temperament, and cultural significance.
DESCRIPTION: Silkie chicks hatch as small, rounded balls of soft down with a notably calm demeanor. Unlike most chickens, their down has a fur-like texture that gives them a plush, toy-like appearance. Early movement is cautious but steady, with chicks staying close to warmth and companions. Silkies mature more slowly than many breeds, developing feathers later in juvenile growth. They imprint readily on handlers and show low stress responses to routine care. Brooding instincts are strong even at a young age, with chicks displaying quiet, settled behavior. Vocalizations are soft and infrequent compared to other breeds. Growth emphasizes fluff and body mass rather than speed or size. Coordination improves gradually as feathers emerge. Social bonding is strong within small groups. Their relaxed nature makes them less reactive to sudden sounds or disturbances. Early handling further reinforces trust and calm behavior.
SIZE: Newly hatched chicks weigh about 1–1.5 oz and reach 1.5–2 lb as adults.
APPEARANCE: Fluffy fur-like down, rounded body, short legs, dark skin, and small beak with dark pigmentation.
TEMPERAMENT: Gentle, calm, friendly, and docile, with low aggression and strong tolerance for handling.
CARE REQUIREMENTS: Require dry bedding, warmth, protection from moisture, gentle handling, and separation from aggressive birds.
LIFESPAN: Silkie chickens typically live 7–9 yrs.
DOMESTIC ROLE: Ornamental poultry, broody foster hen, companion animal, and exhibition bird.
NOTABLE BREEDS / VARIETIES: White, black, blue, buff, partridge, and splash Silkies.
INTERESTING FACTS: Silkies have black skin and bones due to fibromelanosis. Their feathers lack functioning barbicels, preventing flight. Silkies are renowned for brooding and often hatch eggs of other breeds. They have five toes instead of the usual four. Silkie chicks remain fluffy longer than most chickens.

Silkie chicken chick. Illustration copyright © Lochlainn Seabrook.

# TORTOISE

COMMON NAME: Tortoise.
BABY NAME: Hatchling.
SCIENTIFIC NAME: *Testudinidae*.
ANIMAL TYPE: Domestic reptile.
TAXONOMIC ORDER: Testudines.
ORIGIN: Africa, Asia, Europe, and the Americas, with several species long kept in captivity as companion animals.
DESCRIPTION: Baby tortoises hatch fully formed from leathery eggs after an extended incubation period. At birth they are small, alert, and instinctively cautious, relying on camouflage and stillness for protection. Their movements are slow but deliberate, with strong limbs adapted for walking rather than swimming. Hatchlings immediately begin exploring their enclosure, guided by scent and light. Growth is gradual and steady, supported by a high-calcium, plant-based diet. The shell begins relatively soft and hardens as the tortoise matures. Early development focuses on strengthening bones and shell structure. Hatchlings spend much of their time resting between feeding and short periods of exploration. Environmental stability is critical during this stage. Proper humidity and temperature directly affect healthy shell growth.
SIZE: Hatchlings typically measure 1.5–3 in. long and weigh 0.5–2 oz. depending on species.
APPEARANCE: Small domed shell, proportionally large head and eyes, sturdy legs, and a visible yolk scar shortly after hatching.
TEMPERAMENT: Quiet, independent, observant, and calm, with limited social interaction but consistent routines.
CARE REQUIREMENTS: Require controlled heat, UVB lighting, appropriate humidity, calcium-rich diet, and spacious, secure enclosure.
LIFESPAN: Many domestic tortoises live 50–100 yrs or more.
DOMESTIC ROLE: Companion animal, educational animal, and long-term stewardship pet.
NOTABLE BREEDS / VARIETIES: Russian tortoise, Greek tortoise, Hermann's tortoise, sulcata tortoise, and leopard tortoise.
INTERESTING FACTS: Baby tortoises hatch with an egg tooth used to break the shell. Their shells grow in visible scutes over time. Temperature during incubation can influence sex. Hatchlings instinctively seek warmth and light. Tortoises can recognize feeding routines early in life. Some species grow for several decades before reaching full size. Young tortoises can absorb moisture through specialized areas of the shell and skin to aid hydration.

Tortoise hatchling. Illustration copyright © Lochlainn Seabrook.

# TURKEY

COMMON NAME: Turkey.
BABY NAME: Poult.
SCIENTIFIC NAME: *Meleagris gallopavo domesticus*.
ANIMAL TYPE: Domestic bird.
TAXONOMIC ORDER: Galliformes.
ORIGIN: North America, domesticated from the wild turkey by Indigenous peoples for food, feathers, and ceremonial use.
DESCRIPTION: Turkey poults are small, lightweight hatchlings covered in soft down and known for rapid early growth. At hatching they are alert but delicate, requiring warmth and close management. Poults rely heavily on visual cues and quickly learn to follow movement. Their legs strengthen rapidly, allowing confident walking within days. Feeding behavior develops quickly as they learn to peck at food and water. Early life is marked by high metabolic demand and sensitivity to temperature. Poults grow rapidly during the first several weeks, gaining muscle mass and coordination. Social behavior emerges early, with poults forming loose groups and responding to flock dynamics. Human handling during this stage can reduce stress and improve adaptability. Vocalizations are frequent and serve as contact calls when separated.
SIZE: Newly hatched poults weigh about 2–3 oz and may reach 2–3 lb by 6–8 wks of age.
APPEARANCE: Soft yellow, brown, or striped down, small rounded body, proportionally large head, and sturdy developing legs.
TEMPERAMENT: Alert, social, curious, responsive, with strong following behavior, flock awareness, and notable learning ability.
CARE REQUIREMENTS: Require steady warmth, high-protein feed, clean water, dry bedding, and protection from drafts.
LIFESPAN: Domestic turkeys typically live 8–10 yrs.
DOMESTIC ROLE: Livestock bird raised for meat, breeding, education, and small farm settings.
NOTABLE BREEDS / VARIETIES: Broad Breasted White, Broad Breasted Bronze, Bourbon Red, Narragansett, and Royal Palm.
INTERESTING FACTS: Turkey poults imprint strongly on moving objects shortly after hatching. They must be taught to eat and drink during the first days of life. Poults communicate using soft peeps to maintain contact with flock mates. Their rapid growth rate is among the fastest of domestic birds. Poults are very intelligent and can recognize familiar caretakers through repeated exposure.

Turkey poult. Illustration copyright © Lochlainn Seabrook.

# WELSH PONY

COMMON NAME: Welsh pony.
BABY NAME: Foal.
SCIENTIFIC NAME: *Equus ferus caballus*.
ANIMAL TYPE: Domestic mammal.
TAXONOMIC ORDER: Perissodactyla.
ORIGIN: Wales, developed as a hardy mountain pony adapted to rough terrain and cool climates.
DESCRIPTION: Welsh pony foals are small, compact newborns with strong legs and a dense early coat that reflects their rugged heritage. They stand and nurse shortly after birth, displaying quick balance and alert awareness. Early growth emphasizes coordination and muscle tone, allowing foals to follow the mare across uneven ground. Their movement is energetic and springy, with frequent bursts of playful running. Foals bond closely with the mare and show early social awareness within a herd. Curiosity appears quickly, leading to exploration of objects and people. The breed's intelligence is evident in rapid learning and responsiveness. Bone structure develops steadily to support long-term soundness. Foals exhibit stamina beyond their size, often remaining active for extended periods. Early handling encourages confidence and calm behavior.
SIZE: Newborn foals weigh about 60–90 lb and stand 3–3.5 ft tall at the shoulder within weeks.
APPEARANCE: Short, sturdy frame, refined head, large expressive eyes, small ears, and a thick mane and tail.
TEMPERAMENT: Gentle, intelligent, alert, and eager, with a playful yet cooperative disposition.
CARE REQUIREMENTS: Require regular nursing, clean pasture, shelter from extreme weather, hoof care, and early social handling.
LIFESPAN: Welsh ponies typically live 25–30 yrs.
DOMESTIC ROLE: Riding pony for children, driving pony, show animal, and companion animal.
NOTABLE BREEDS / VARIETIES: Section A Welsh Mountain Pony, Section B Riding Pony, Section C Cob Type, and Section D Welsh Cob.
INTERESTING FACTS: Welsh pony foals often show strong jumping ability at a young age. The breed is known for exceptional longevity and soundness. Foals develop thick coats suited for cold climates. Their intelligence makes early training especially effective. Welsh ponies have influenced many modern pony breeds worldwide, contributing to athleticism and temperament traits.

Welsh pony foal. Illustration copyright © Lochlainn Seabrook.

# YAK

COMMON NAME: Yak.
BABY NAME: Calf.
SCIENTIFIC NAME: *Bos grunniens*.
ANIMAL TYPE: Domestic mammal.
TAXONOMIC ORDER: Artiodactyla.
ORIGIN: Central Asia, domesticated on the Tibetan Plateau for transport, milk, fiber, meat, and fuel.
DESCRIPTION: Yak calves are sturdy, thick-coated newborns adapted from birth to cold, high-altitude environments. They are born with strong legs and are able to stand and nurse shortly after birth. Early growth is steady rather than rapid, supporting endurance and long-term strength. Calves remain close to their mothers, relying on constant contact for warmth and protection. Their dense hair begins developing immediately, providing insulation against wind and snow. Yak calves are highly alert and quickly learn to follow herd movement patterns. Coordination improves within weeks as they navigate uneven terrain. Social bonds form early with both mothers and herd members. Their behavior is calm and deliberate, conserving energy in harsh conditions. Development favors resilience over speed.
SIZE: Newborn calves weigh about 25–35 lb and reach 150–200 lb by 6 mos of age.
APPEARANCE: Compact body, long shaggy hair, rounded muzzle, small ears, and dark expressive eyes.
TEMPERAMENT: Calm, gentle, cautious, and strongly bonded to the mother, with low reactivity.
CARE REQUIREMENTS: Require maternal nursing, cold-tolerant shelter, clean grazing areas, and minimal stress.
LIFESPAN: Domestic yaks typically live 20–25 yrs.
DOMESTIC ROLE: Livestock animal used for milk, fiber, hides, leather, transport, and subsistence farming.
NOTABLE BREEDS / VARIETIES: Tibetan yak, Mongolian yak, Himalayan yak, and hybrid dzo varieties.
INTERESTING FACTS: Yak calves are born with larger lungs adapted for thin air. Their thick coats begin forming within days. Calves can tolerate freezing temperatures better than many adult cattle. They instinctively conserve energy rather than engage in frequent play. Yak calves vocalize softly to maintain contact with their mothers. Their hair later becomes one of the world's warmest natural fibers. Yak calves develop thick underwool early in life, which later becomes the soft fiber known as yak down.

Yak calf. Illustration copyright © Lochlainn Seabrook.

# YORKSHIRE TERRIER

COMMON NAME: Yorkshire terrier.
BABY NAME: Puppy.
SCIENTIFIC NAME: *Canis lupus familiaris*.
ANIMAL TYPE: Domestic mammal.
TAXONOMIC ORDER: Carnivora.
ORIGIN: England, developed in the 19$^{th}$ Century for ratting in mills and mines, later refined as a companion breed.
DESCRIPTION: Yorkshire terrier puppies are extremely small, fine-boned, and compact at birth, with soft coats and proportionally large heads. Early development emphasizes alertness and responsiveness rather than size. Puppies are energetic and quick to move once mobile, displaying strong confidence despite their tiny stature. Coordination improves rapidly during the first weeks as balance and agility emerge. Vocalization is frequent, serving both communication and attention-seeking. Yorkie puppies form strong bonds with caregivers early and thrive on close human contact. Their intelligence shows quickly through problem-solving and responsiveness to training cues. Play behavior is lively and persistent, often exceeding expectations for such a small dog. Curiosity drives exploration, especially toward sounds and movement. Early socialization strongly influences long-term temperament and adaptability.
SIZE: Newborn puppies weigh about 3–4 oz and reach 2–4 lb by 12 wks of age.
APPEARANCE: Small frame, erect ears, dark eyes, short muzzle, and a fine, silky coat that develops texture with age.
TEMPERAMENT: Bold, alert, affectionate, confident, and highly attached to caregivers.
CARE REQUIREMENTS: Require warmth, frequent meals, gentle handling, grooming, early training, and close supervision.
LIFESPAN: Yorkshire terriers typically live 13–16 yrs.
DOMESTIC ROLE: Companion animal, toy breed, and alert household dog.
NOTABLE BREEDS / VARIETIES: Traditional Yorkshire terrier, parti-color Yorkshire terrier, and teacup-size lines.
INTERESTING FACTS: Yorkshire terrier puppies are born with black-and-tan coats that lighten as they mature. They often show fearless behavior disproportionate to their size. The breed descends from several small terriers used for vermin control. Yorkies retain strong prey instincts despite being companion dogs. Puppies can learn basic commands at an early age. Their silky coat more closely resembles human hair than typical animal fur.

Yorkshire terrier puppy. Illustration copyright © Lochlainn Seabrook.

*The End*

# MEET THE AUTHOR

LOCHLAINN SEABROOK is a prolific lifelong researcher, historian, author, artist, and composer whose knowledge and experience span numerous fields. His remarkable productivity stems from his broad interests, decades of meticulous research, and an unwavering daily devotion to writing and creative exploration.

The idea of specializing in a single subject is a modern invention. In the spirit of the great polymaths—Aristotle, Isaac Newton, Benjamin Franklin, and Thomas Jefferson—Seabrook works across dozens of disciplines, with intellectual pursuits encompassing history, science, philosophy, religion, and the arts. The result is an expansive body of original writings that distill years of careful analysis into clear, accessible language for the general reader.

Rejecting the narrow confines of modern specialization, Seabrook views all knowledge as intrinsically interconnected. This integrative vision, combined with long hours of focused, solitary study and a rigorous work ethic, has enabled him to produce an extraordinary corpus of literature uniting the sciences and the humanities—a natural outgrowth of a lifetime devoted to inquiry, creativity, and the preservation of evidence-based history.

AMERICAN POLYMATH LOCHLAINN SEABROOK is a bestselling author, award-winning historian, and acclaimed multidisciplinary artist. A descendant of the families of Alexander Hamilton Stephens, John Singleton Mosby, Edmund Winchester Rucker, and William Giles Harding, the neo-Victorian scholar is a 7th generation Kentuckian, and one of the most prolific and widely read traditional writers in the world today. Known by literary critics as the "new Shelby Foote," the "American Robert Graves," the "Southern Joseph Campbell,"

and the "Rocky Mountain Richard Jefferies," and by his fans as the "the best author ever," he is a recipient of the United Daughters of the Confederacy's prestigious Jefferson Davis Historical Gold Medal, and is considered the foremost Southern interpreter of American Civil War history—or what he refers to as the War for the Constitution (1861-1865).

A lifelong litterateur, the Sons of Confederate Veterans member has authored and edited books ranging in topics from ancient and modern history, politics, science, comparative religion, diet and nutrition, spirituality, astronomy, entertainment, military, biography, mysticism, anthropology, cryptozoology, photography, and Bible studies, to natural history, technology, paleography, music, humor, gastronomy, etymology, paleontology, onomastics, mysteries, alternative health and fitness, wildlife, alternate history, comparative mythology, genealogy, Christian history, and the paranormal; books that his readers describe as "game changers," "transformative," and "life altering."

One of America's most popular living historians, nature writers, autodidacts, and Transcendentalists, he is a 17th generation Southerner of Appalachian heritage who descends from dozens of patriotic Revolutionary War soldiers and Confederate soldiers from Kentucky, Tennessee, North Carolina, and Virginia. Also a history, wildlife, and nature preservationist, the well-respected scrivener began life as a child prodigy, later maturing into an archetypal Renaissance Man and classical polymath.

Besides being cofounder and co-CEO of Sea Raven Press, an accomplished writer, author, historian, biographer, lexicographer, encyclopedist, neologist, publisher, editor, poet, polymathic creative, onomastician, etymologist, and Bible authority, the influential prosateur is also a Kentucky Colonel, eagle scout, entrepreneur, businessman, composer, screenwriter, nature, wildlife, and landscape photographer, videographer, and filmmaker, artist, artisan, painter, watercolorist, sculptor, ceramic artist, visual artist, sketch artist, pen and ink artist, graphic artist, graphic designer, book designer, book formatter, editorial designer, book cover designer, publishing designer, Web designer, poster artist, digital artist, cartoonist, content creator, inventor, aquarist, genealogist, ufologist, jewelry designer, jewelry maker, former history museum docent, teacher's assistant, and a former Red Cross certified lifeguard, ranch hand, zookeeper, and wrangler. A contemporary songwriter (of some 3,000 songs in a dozen genres), he is also a pianist, organist, drummer, bass player, rhythm guitarist, rhythm mandolinist, percussionist, electronic musician, synthesist, clavichordist, harpsichordist, classical composer, jingle composer, film composer (currently his musical work has been featured in 11 movies), lyricist, band leader, multi-instrument musician, lead vocalist, backup vocalist, session player, music producer, and recording studio mixing engineer, who has worked and performed with some of Nashville's top musicians and singers.

Currently Seabrook is the multi-genre author and editor of over 100 adult and children's books (totaling some 30,000 pages and 15,000,000 words) that have earned him accolades from around the globe. His works, which have sold on every continent except Antarctica, have introduced hundreds of thousands to vital facts that have been left out of our mainstream books. He has been endorsed internationally by leading experts, museum curators, award-winning historians, chart-topping authors, celebrities, filmmakers, noted scientists, well regarded educators, TV show hosts and producers, renowned military artists, venerable heritage organizations, and distinguished academicians of all races, creeds, and colors.

He currently holds two interesting world records: He is the author of the most books on American military officer Nathan Bedford Forrest, and he was the first to publicize and describe the 19th-Century platform reversal of America's two main political parties, namely that Civil War era Democrats (primarily in the South—the Confederacy) were Conservatives, while Civil War era Republicans (primarily in the North—the Union) were Liberals.

Of northern, western, and central European ancestry, he is the 6th great-grandson of the Earl of Oxford and a descendant of European royalty through his Kentucky father and West Virginia mother. A proud descendant of Appalachian coal miners, trainmen, mountain folk, and wilderness pioneers, his modern day cousins include: Johnny Cash, Elvis Presley, Lisa Marie Presley, Billy Ray and Miley Cyrus, Patty Loveless, Tim McGraw, Lee Ann Womack, Dolly Parton, Pat Boone, Naomi, Wynonna, and Ashley Judd, Ricky Skaggs, the Sunshine Sisters, Martha Carson, Chet Atkins, Patrick J. Buchanan, Cindy Crawford, Bertram Thomas Combs (Kentucky's 50th governor), Edith Bolling (second wife of President Woodrow Wilson), Andy Griffith, Riley Keough, George C. Scott, Robert Duvall, Reese Witherspoon, Lee Marvin, Rebecca Gayheart, and Tom Cruise.

A constitutionalist, avid outdoorsman, wilderness conservationist, and gun rights advocate, Seabrook is the author of the international blockbuster, *Everything You Were Taught About the Civil War is Wrong, Ask a Southerner!* He lives with his wife and family in the magnificent Rocky Mountains, heart of the American West, where you will find him writing, hiking, and filming.

*For more information on Mr. Seabrook visit*
**LochlainnSeabrook.com**

# Praise for Author-Historian-Artist Lochlainn Seabrook

"Bestselling author, award-winning historian, and esteemed nature writer Lochlainn Seabrook straddles multiple genres with ease, seamlessly weaving together history, science, politics, philosophy, and spirituality with the authority of a scholar and the flair of a storyteller." — SEA RAVEN PRESS

### COMMENTS FROM OUR READERS AROUND THE WORLD

✯ "Lochlainn Seabrook is a genius writer!" — STEVEN WARD
✯ "Best author ever." — EMILY
✯ "We get asked a lot what books we use and read. We don't do many modern historians, but we make an exception for some, and Lochlainn Seabrook is one of them. His works are completely well researched from original documents, and heavily footnoted and documented." — SOUTHERN HISTORICAL SOCIETY
✯ "Looking forward to more Lochlainn Seabrook books, my favourite historian!" — ALBERTO IGLESIAS
✯ "Lochlainn Seabrook is one of the finest authors on true history in this century. His books should be on every student's desk." — RONDA SAMMONS RENO
✯ "All of Col. Seabrook's books are great. I have bought most of them and want to end up buying them all." — DAVID VAUGHN
✯ "Lochlainn pulls together such arcane facts with relative ease, compiling these into ordinary prose that strike to the heart with substance, no fluff-speak. I am awestruck! Really. He is an inspiration to me. . . . He is truly a revolutionist. He dares to speak what others whisper; he writes with a boldness and an authoritative knowledge that is second to none." — JAY KRUIZENGA
✯ "Mr. Lochlainn Seabrook is . . . the most well researched and heavily documented author I've ever read. His books are must haves. Everything he writes should be required reading! I assure you, you won't be disappointed. One simply cannot go wrong with his books. Mr. Seabrook is awesome! . . . I have never read any other author as well researched and footnoted as him. I've been in love with Mr. Seabrook for almost 5 years now. His quick wit and logic is enough reason to purchase his books. But the mere fact that he's so extensively researched is icing on the cake. Mr. Seabrook is my favorite, hands down." — LANI BURNETTE RINKEL
✯ "My favorite book is the Bible. Lochlainn Seabrook wrote my second favorite book." — RICHARD FINGER
✯ "I have a new favorite author and his name is Lochlainn Seabrook." — J. EWING
✯ "Lochlainn Seabrook is an incredible writer and I love all of his books on the South. . . . His writing is brilliant. . . . I look forward to reading more of his masterpieces. Thank you." — JOEY
✯ "It's hard to choose just one of Lochlainn's books!" — ROSANNE STEELE
✯ "Mr. Seabrook, thank you ever so much for blessing us with your most enlightening works." — LAURENCE DRURY
✯ "I recommend anything written by Lochlainn Seabrook." — HOTRODMOB
✯ "Awesome books . . . by a great writer of truth, Lochlainn. Thank you so much. Keep up the great work you do." — WILDBUNCH19INF
✯ "I love Lochlainn Seabrook's style and approach. It's not the 'norm.' What a miracle his books are. . . . He is a literal life changing author! Amazing books!" — KEITH PARISH

✯ "I adore Mr. Seabrook's style and I love his books. I love an author that does proper research, and still finds a way to engage the reader. Mr. Seabrook does an admirable job of both." — DONALD CAUL

✯ "Lochlainn Seabrook's books are much more well researched and authoritative than those eminently celebrated as being the authorities on the subjects he writes on. You can always trust to find the truth in his writings. . . . He does not rewrite history, but instead shows it as it is." — GARY STIER
✯ "I love all of Colonel Seabrook's books. They are informative and enlightening, and his warm Southern hospitality writing style makes you feel right at home." — KEITH CRAVEN
✯ "Lochlainn Seabrook's work is an absolute treasure of scholarship and historic scope." — MARK WAYNE CUNNINGHAM
✯ "Mr. Seabrook's command of . . . history is breathtaking. . . . He deserves great renown—check out his books!" — MARGARET SIMMONS
✯ "I love Seabrook's writings. LOVE!!! . . . So grateful to know the truth! Keep writing Lochlainn!!!" — REBECCA DALRYMPLE
✯ "Lochlainn Seabrook . . . [has] probably [written] the best book on mental science in existence by a living author. Along with Thomas Troward, Emmet Fox, and Jack Addington, Mr. Seabrook is one of the top four mental science authors of all time, since biblical times." - IAN BARTON STEWART
✯ "Glad I discovered Mr. Seabrook! . . . He writes eye opening books! Unbelievable the facts he unearths - and he backs it all up with truth, notes, footnotes, and bibliography! . . . He always amazes me! His books always see the whole picture. His timelines and bibliographies are incredible. He always provides carefully reasoned arguments! He's the best. To me I think he's better than the late great Shelby Foote! America needs more like Lochlainn Seabrook. I can't wait to own all of his books on the war someday. Everyone who wants the Truth, who seeks the Truth and wants the full story, should read his books." — JOHN BULL BADER
✯ "I love all of Colonel Seabrook's books!" — DEBBIE SIDLE
✯ "Amazing books for unreconstructed people who actually want to know the TRUTH. Seabrook's skill in writing and researching has no equal since the great Shelby Foote. If I could rate his books more than five stars I would." — CANDICE
✯ "Lochlainn Seabrook is well educated and versed in what he writes and I'm impressed with the delivery." — THOMAS L. WHITE
✯ "Lochlainn Seabrook is the author of great works of scholarship." — JOHN B.
✯ "Thank you Lochlainn Seabrook for your wonderful books! You are the real deal! You are an amazing author and I love your books!!" — SOPHIA MEOW CELLIST
✯ "I really enjoy Mr. Seabrook's books! His knowledge is beyond belief!" — SANDRA FISH
✯ "Love Lochlainn Seabrook. Awesome!!" — ROBIN HENDERSON ARISTIDES
✯ "Kudos to Lochlainn Seabrook who is a very good and informative professional truthful historian. We need more like him!" — AMY VACHON

*Nurture Your Mind, Body, and Spirit!*

READ THE BOOKS OF

# SEA RAVEN PRESS

Visit our Webstore for a wide selection of wholesome, family-friendly, evidence-based, educational books for all ages. You'll be glad you did!

*Artisan-Crafted Books & Merch From the Rocky Mountains*

THANK YOU FOR SUPPORTING OUR SMALL AMERICAN FAMILY BUSINESS!

# SeaRavenPress.com

Visit our sister sites:
LochlainnSeabrook.com
YouTube.com/user/SeaRavenPress
YouTube.com/@SeabrookFilms
Rumble.com/user/SeaRavenPress
Pond5.com/artist/LochlainnSeabrook

If you enjoyed this book you will be interested in some of Colonel Seabrook's popular related titles:

- The 50 Cutest Wild Baby Animals in the World: An Illustrated Guide to Our Planet's Most Adorable Young Wildlife
- The 50 Greatest Sharks of All Time: A Visual Guide to the Ocean's Apex Predators
- When Monsters Ruled: The 25 Scariest Animals of the Prehistoric World
- The 50 Most Beautiful Aquarium Fish in the World: An Illustrated Guide to Nature's Most Stunning Freshwater and Marines Species
- Rocky Mountain Equines: A Photographic Collection of Horses, Donkeys, and Mules of the American West
- Rocky Mountain Bison: A Photographic Collection of Bison of the American West
- The Cryptid Files Unsealed: An Illustrated Guide to the World's Most Terrifying Unknown Creatures
- The Concise Book of Owls: A Guide to Nature's Most Mysterious Birds
- North America's Amazing Mammals: An Encyclopedia for the Whole Family

Available from Sea Raven Press and wherever fine books are sold.

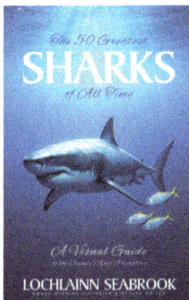

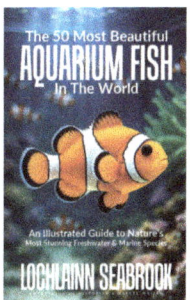

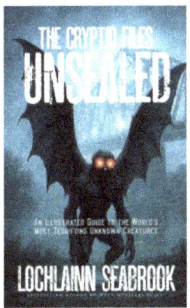

PLEASE VISIT OUR WEBSTORE FOR A COMPLETE LIST OF COLONEL SEABROOK'S BOOKS, AS WELL AS HIS FINE ART NATURE & WILDLIFE PHOTO PRINTS, WALL POSTERS, AND BUMPER STICKERS

## SeaRavenPress.com

www.ingramcontent.com/pod-product-compliance
Lightning Source LLC
Chambersburg PA
CBHW040304170426
43194CB00021B/2889